The Caravan Chronicles

Matthew Klem

Published by Matthew Klem / Magestik Publishing

Copyright © 2019 Matthew Klem / Magestik Publishing

All rights reserved

www.caravan-chronicles.com

All rights reserved.

No part of this book may be reproduced or transmitted in any form or by any means without the written permission of the publisher and author.

Some names and other identifying features of individuals portrayed in this book have been changed. Other individual's real names are used with explicit permission from them.

Photo credits: Matthew Klem, Paul Steeves, Ken Arsenault, Mark Knowles

Newspaper article courtesy of The Times & Transcript

Front and Rear Cover Artwork courtesy of Norm Delaney

Map images provided by Google Maps © 2019 Google, INEGI

Geocaching.com © 2019 Groundspeak Inc.

ISBN: 978-0-9865081-3-4

DEDICATION

To my son Dylan who reminded me it doesn't matter what anyone else thinks.

Table of Contents

Preface 5
Finding a New Adventure 9
Just Keep on Going 31
Are We There Yet? 49
From Milestones to Giants 67
No Time Like Our Own 96
The Earth, The Skies & Cars Disguised 117
Move Along Nothing to See Here 131
From Traveler to Local in One Ride 139
The Longest Journey 149
The Aftermath 157
APPENDIX I – Geocache List 163
APPENDIX II – Notable Cities / Our Route 171

Preface

> Where I give the lowdown on where and how this book came to be.

Preface

During this trip, I had a journal where I was making notes about anything significant that we encountered. Often I would forget to jot something down and would come back to it at a later time that day or even later along the trip. During the trek home, Paul and I spoke about the things I had written down, and I had said I intended to do a nice lengthy write-up about the trip for our website. What he didn't know at the time was that there were two reasons for me wanting to take so many notes about the trip.

It was always my intention to sit down and write out as much detail as I could about our journey and experiences we had while traveling across the United States. Whether it was in a single blog post on our website or a series of posts on another blog, I knew that I had to put it down while it was still fresh. As time passes, the minutia of each one of those days gets harder to recall. I wanted to make sure that much like many of the other big trips I had taken, there was a written account somewhere that I could go back to and remind myself of what had happened. But along with just wanting to write it down for posterity, a part of me thought that maybe there would be enough material to write an entire book.

Before the trip, I had finished the first draft of another book I had written about many of my other travel experiences around the world. With the bulk of that book now behind me, I was looking for my next big writing project. But honestly, by the time the trip was over and I reviewed my notes, I started to wonder if there was enough material to write a book at all.

So I decided I would sit down and write whatever I could remember and then decide what to do with it later. As I started writing pieces here and there, I would post little snippets to Facebook to gauge a little bit of the reaction. During outings with Paul, he'd often ask me how my write-up was going, and I'd tell him that it's a work in progress. By the time I got through to the end, I had realized there was just too much here to post as a blog entry, and so The Caravan Chronicles was born.

For those who have never heard of, or know very little about the hobby of geocaching, don't let that hold you back from perusing the pages that follow. Everything you need to know about the hobby as it applies to this trip is within these chapters. And for those of you who have signed a log, written a TFTC somewhere, or have said "just one more…" while out in the wild, you'll recognize some of our antics and relate to some of our woes.

But no matter who you are, I hope this story puts a smile on your face and maybe inspires you to take a road trip somewhere.

Finding a New Adventure

> Why we chose to take on a crazy road trip like this and how geocaching led us to it.

Driving along a red dirt road, one of the boys yells out that we are getting closer. Ron pulls the car over, and all four of us head into the woods. The bush here was incredibly thick. Spruce trees surrounded each of us within moments of entering the wooded area, and before we knew it, no one could see anything except the branches of whatever tree happened to smack you in your face.

"I'm at Ground Zero, but I got nothing" from one voice.

"Mine's just spinning. Any luck?" another asks.

Known as the "drunken bee dance," the four of us had engaged in a relatively common practice of walking circles around the same area looking for the same thing. Examining every branch, and every limb of every tree we spotted, no one was coming up with the find. The hint itself seemed incredibly simple, and the name of the geocache seemingly gave it away. We suspected it was small as much of what we had found earlier could easily fit in your hand. But just as I was about to call it and tell the boys to move on to the next one, I hear Paul's voice.

"I've got it!" Paul squawked with a bit of joy in his voice.

We all had a small sigh of relief and started to head back towards the car.

"You guys have got to see this," he said. The name of what we were looking for was "Another micro in the woods" (GC1GVCM) and given that the term "micro" depicts the container to be small enough to fit in your hand, I cast my doubts on whether or not it made much sense to see yet another film canister in a tree. But we all knew that Paul wouldn't have grabbed our attention for something so simple. The rest of us made our way through the trees, following his voice until eventually, we came upon the "micro" he had found in the woods.

Sitting along the branch of one of the smaller spruce trees was a microwave oven. An actual microwave oven, in the middle of the woods, hanging from a tree was the "micro" we had been looking for. Inside the oven was a tobacco canister that had the log sheet, and all four of us started laughing. Someone snapped a picture of Ken beside the microwave before we all signed the log, put the container back in the oven, and kept on moving. The misdirection of the name combined with the hilarious idea of a microwave in a tree have made that geocache stand out as one of my all-time favorites in the 12 years that I have been geocaching.

For the next four years, all four of us would return to PEI on that same weekend to go geocaching. Through the course of Friday evening, all of Saturday, and part of Sunday, we would have our heads buried in a GPS, looking at maps, and finding countless pill bottles hanging in trees across the likes of Prince Edward Island. Sure, now and then, we'd find something unique like a microwave oven, but more often than not, it was bottles upon bottles hanging in trees. But that trip also served as yet another beginning for me.

Despite some of the repetitive finds during our weekend away, it never seemed to matter. It wasn't the actual geocaching that made the trip fun. It was the banter in the car which included countless insults to each other, Paul's meticulous planning for the route we would take to get as many caches as possible, to Ron's laid back attitude when he'd often spent more time in the car doing the driving and putting up with us than doing any geocaching. In the end, it was all about four friends who had connected through geocaching, enjoying a weekend away to have some fun.

Geocaching is a "high tech treasure hunt" using a GPS or mobile device to find containers that have been hidden all around the world. Once found, you sign your name on the "log" sheet and place the container back where you found it for the next person to find. Almost every country across the globe has geocaches hidden somewhere within its borders. Whether it's across the street from your house or at the south pole, geocaches are everywhere. The hobby knows no boundary of age, size, sex, religion, color, or political affiliation. It's an activity that anyone can participate in. Given the broad nature of the way people participate in the hobby, there's something in it for everyone. Some try it out and enjoy it for a while, then move on to the next big thing. Those who stick it out often end up part of a broader community. In joining a large group like this, it often leads to great friendships and great experiences, much like my repeated trips to PEI with three guys I met through geocaching.

I had started geocaching in late 2007, and by the time 2013 had rolled around, I found myself neck-deep in everything geocaching. Hosting events, hiding containers, forming a geocaching organization to help promote the hobby in our region, and eventually having a big hand in putting on the first geocaching "mega" event (a geocaching event with 500+ attendees) in Moncton back in 2015 all topped my geocaching resume. Geocaching had become an integral part of my life. But when August 1st, 2015 rolled around, and the M3 mega-event went off better than we had expected, the excitement of geocaching for me had finally begun to wane.

In my early days of caching, the idea of using a GPS enabled device to find a container hidden either somewhere in the woods or creatively camouflaged within the city was captivating to me. I spent hours upon hours searching for these containers all over the town I happened to be visiting. But through the course of learning more about geocaching, I found an entire community of people who were as obsessed with the hobby as I had become. It turns out that for me, the best part of geocaching wasn't so much the rush of finding the container, but the comradery you experienced being out with a group of people who shared a similar interest.

By the time the mega had come and gone, I had found myself less and less interested in spending time trying to find film canisters in trees or Tupperware under rocks. As much as the hobby excited me at one time, after eight years of mostly finding the same things again and again, the appeal had dissipated considerably. But I had made some terrific friends through geocaching, and every time we went out as a group, I always found myself thoroughly enjoying the experience. It made me realize that I was no longer interested in geocaching alone and just wanted to spend more time with good people.

At some point later on after the mega, I asked my good friend Ken Arsenault if he was interested in getting a few people together to make a geocaching trip somewhere down in the US. I had met Ken in April of 2008 at a geocaching event he had held. It was the first event I had ever been to, and it exposed me to the more social aspect of geocaching. I had helped Ken get his internet access working at the event, and we struck up a good conversation. In August of that same year, he invited me to go with him and two other cachers to a mega event in Quebec City. I didn't know any of the other guys, but it seemed like a fun road trip, so away I went. Ken and I became pretty good friends after that, and then starting in 2009, we began those yearly trips over to PEI with Ron & Paul.

If someone asked you to sit down and try to describe one of your friends to them, depending on the person, it may or may not be all that easy. In the time that I have known Ken, he's always been an avid outdoorsman which is what I suspect got him roped into geocaching. From going fishing out on his boat to hiking, hammocking, and hunting, Ken seems to be someone who enjoys being in the middle of nowhere. But almost as much as he loves the outdoors, Ken is a guy who revels in a good conversation. We've recorded more than 50hrs worth of podcasts, and each time we'd sit down and talk, we'd barely notice that an hour had passed. As the bar manager at a private club back home, Ken is the perfect guy to be behind the bar, serving drinks, and talking to anyone who comes in. Combine that with his sarcastic sense of humor, and a good family life, he's a guy that can get along with just about anyone.

Ken was up for going on an excursion down to the US as long as we made sure anyone coming with us wouldn't drive us crazy. It had been four years since we had made our last PEI trip with Ron and Paul. Although we all kept in touch, both of them had fallen out of geocaching, so it was far less likely they'd be interested in going on a much longer trek down into the USA. So the search was on to find two other people we could handle spending 14 days with. I suggested Paul Steeves & Jason Perkins as travel companions, and Ken immediately agreed.

Like any social group, geocachers run the gamut when it comes to personality types, but if you attend any of the significant events, you can sometimes spot a bit of a pattern. There are a lot of unique people that follow this hobby, but by far and large, geocachers are pretty decent individuals. But still, to spend a lot of time in a car or plane with others, you need to make sure they won't drive you crazy.

Paul and Jason were two geocachers we both had known for quite a while. Again, like any social circle, you can usually pick out the ones that are on the same wavelength as yourself. I think that's why Ken and I became good friends. Paul & Jason were two other examples of people we just got along with without having to even think about it. Both of them were on the organizing committee for the mega, and although we had known them for a while before that, doing so much work on that event helped us all get to know one another even more.

I'd become more familiar with Jason through geocaching, mainly because he tended to help out quite a bit at many of the events I was attending. A family man, I would often see Jason with one of his kids at various events. We both shared an oddball sense of humor and got along quite well. He also tended to be a bit more analytical about specific topics when we'd get into the planning phases of both this trip and other things we were involved in together. He would often point out perspectives that others hadn't considered, which made him an even better fit for this little excursion.

For me, I'd best describe Paul as the quiet one amongst the four of us. Not as loud or sarcastic as Ken, and wouldn't often say too much to ruffle feathers, but again was a good standing family man with a history of loving the outdoors as well. Paul would tell many stories about "being up at the camp" or out hunting with his friends. But despite his quiet demeanor, I came to find Paul quite hysterical when he had his moments. Comments or jokes that would seem to come out of nowhere would immediately put a huge smile on my face. Often Jason would crack up at the little things coming out of Paul as we'd be hiking on a trail trying to find more geocaches.

Having gotten to know these guys over the last few years made it easier to pitch the idea of a road trip like this to them. They were immediately on board. We hadn't decided where we were going to go, but we knew we wanted to make a trip south of the border as that was the easiest place for us to get to. It also allowed us to snag caches in places we had rarely visited, if ever. So now it was a matter of figuring out exactly when, where, and how we were going to get there.

At first, we thought about hitting up somewhere in the southern states, perhaps down near Louisiana. Pick one state, fly into the nearest airport and cache around the area, and hit up a few more states in the vicinity. We talked a bit about maybe doing some of the national parks. A frequent target for many who go into the US for geocaching is the infamous "ET Highway" powertrail. In geocaching, powertrails refer to a specific trail or roadway where geocaches have been hidden every point one mile (or 161 meters) for the entire length of the trail, or at least a considerable portion of it. These are often sought out by geocachers as they can acquire a large number of finds typically within a short time. Although geocaching does not involve actual competition, some people perceive their "find count," or total number of geocaches they have ever found, as their score. Powertrails offer the ability to bump up one's numbers quite quickly, which is why they are often sought out by those who are a bit more competitive.

The "ET" powertrail consists of 1500 geocaches hidden along highway 375 in rural Nevada. For some geocachers, this trail is seen as a bit of a unique type of challenge in that many seek it out and attempt to beat the record for the fastest time to find all 1500 of the containers. Many others see it as a colossal waste of time and would instead go caching in far more exciting places. I had done a few caches on that road, but neither Ken nor I had much of an interest in trying to do that entire stretch as it can become monotonous after a few hours. So with that trail crossed off the list of potential targets, we continued to ponder where we would end up.

By the time the spring of 2016 had come along, we hadn't made any progress on deciding where we would go or when. Then there was news about this group in the US who were planning to do all 48 states within a single week. They had expected to travel by camper and mainly drive the entire time with only a couple of very strategic stops along the way. Their website didn't give a lot of information about how they were going to do it, but before we knew it, the week had passed, and sure enough, they had accomplished their trip. But alas, after taking on such a journey, their website had gone stale very quickly with no news or stories about how the trip had gone. We never really did find out exactly how it went, but the journey itself did pique our interest.

Both Ken and I thought it was kind of insane to do it in a week, but then Ken made a throwaway comment about maybe we could do it in two weeks and do a bit of site-seeing while on the road. Initially, I didn't think anything of it. But the more it sat with me, the more it sounded like a fantastic opportunity to see a whole lot of a single country in a short window of time. It had started as a joke but quickly turned serious as we began to think about if this was what we wanted to do. We posed the idea to Paul & Jason and as crazy as it sounded, they too were interested in trying to make it happen.

On July 1st, 2016, while our wives were out enjoying the fireworks on the beach, Ken and I sat in the living room with my laptop hooked up to the TV, and we worked out the first version of how our "route" would look. Back and forth we went that night as we figured out the best way to try and hit all 48 states and four Canadian provinces all in a single trip. By the time the night had finished we had plotted a reasonably decent route that would take us from Moncton to North Dakota via the New England states, and then north up into Manitoba, straight west towards Alberta, dip down south to get Wyoming, through Montana and Washington state with a quick corner catch for BC, down to Vegas, and then back east via Texas and New York City. We shared the route with the other guys and started making plans for when we would go.

Timing on a trip like this would make or break it. We needed to be able to travel during a time of year when we were all available, and when the tourism season was low. Going in the middle of the summer was not ideal for any of us as we wanted to make good use of the warm months for our enjoyment while we had them. Weather also played a factor as we didn't want to be in certain parts of the US during the hottest time of the year, as it would make sitting in that car for extended periods even more uncomfortable. Further to that, we also didn't want to be doing any driving in the middle of winter, or a time of year with a lot of rain. We ultimately decided that Labour Day weekend would serve as the perfect time to start a trip like this. It was one less vacation day we would have to take off, and tourist season was over, school was back in session, and so most places would have far less traffic and people out and about during that time of the year. September 3rd, 2017, would serve as the start of our trip. Setting the date and then telling people it was now happening set the ball in motion, and now it was a matter of waiting about a year before we'd leave.

With our departure date now set, and knowing the route we wanted to take, now it became a matter of trying to determine precisely how far we would have to go during each day, and when the breaks would be. Now that we knew when we were leaving, it was vital to try and figure out as carefully as possible where we would be each day of the trip so that we could hit all of the states we wanted, as well as any hotspots we craved to visit.

Google Maps provided all the information that was needed to best estimate what it would take to go from one location to another. Typically I would plot the route from one city to another and then manually adjust it to make sure that it landed in the places we needed to go. For example, if I told Google Maps that I wanted to go from Moncton to Chicago, it would route us through Boston along the I-90, but we needed to go through Vermont, which meant taking some side highways.

Google is good at estimating driving times, but I knew that we'd need to stop for gas, food, and the actual finding of geocaches along the way. I divided the trip into "legs," which were mostly just different sections of the overall trip. The plan was to leave on

Sunday and drive to the middle of Maine and then start the actual first leg of the journey on Monday morning, where we'd go straight from Maine to Chicago and then take a small break there.

Over the course of the next few weeks, I would tweak the route and adjust the timing accordingly. If Google said a leg was going to take 20hrs, I'd mark it as 23-24hrs. I knew that if it took less time, we'd simply just keep driving along the way. The route was looking pretty good, but then Jason brought up one significant point: Did we really need to do the Canadian provinces?

I wanted to get Saskatchewan and Manitoba as I had not found caches in those provinces, and it would have provided all of us the ability to say we had snagged geocaches from one end of the country to the other as we had already found caches in the eastern provinces. But Jason mentioned something about the crossing of the borders that was somewhat concerning and would ultimately change the shape of our trek.

We would have to cross the US/Canada border multiple times to get those provinces. We'd cross into the US from Canada into the state of Maine from our home province of New Brunswick. Then in North Dakota, we'd be making a second border crossing back into Canada for less than a day only to pop back into Montana then back up into Canada for our B.C. cache then returning back to the US.

Coming into Maine was never going to be an issue, but going back into Canada, then back to the US, then back to Canada, and then back to the US again was very likely going to set off a red flag.

We'd probably get stuck at a border and have to try to explain ourselves repeatedly what we were doing and risk not being able to return to the US during one of the crossings. Although I really wanted to get those two other provinces, we all agreed that it made a lot more sense for us just to try and do those provinces on another trip. The route got adjusted again, and instead, we would go straight east through North Dakota and Montana all the way to Washington State.

In late 2016, I registered the domain 4guysinacar.com and created a website that would house all of our adventures. The intention was to use the site as a means for all of us guys to post updated content while on the road. I loaded up profiles of all four of us and even wrote some code to show a map of our route, the geocaches we would find, and also a means to track us almost live while on the road. We got a really cool logo made, and as the summer approached, we were getting a lot more excited.

The route had been more or less finalized after having been tweaked again and again and again. We had worked out a budget of about $2,000 for each person. That money would cover all of the meals, tolls, hotels, and the cost of the vehicle. Yes, the car. This, in itself, was also an interesting discussion.

We had all decided that it made more sense to actually rent a vehicle of some kind than to drive one of our own. But we also knew that we'd be returning the car with 17,000 kilometers on it and that a rental company might frown upon that. We all wondered if the "unlimited mileage" they offer on rental cars would be applicable in a situation like this. Ken managed to get the folks at Enterprise to agree to give us a vehicle with no worries about mileage. He was clear with them about how far we were going to go, and they were okay with it. I did my own digging with Avis, and the manager there just told me flat out, "No. Can't help you." This was in spite of the "unlimited mileage" they seem to offer. We worked out the cost of the gas, and I made a few hotel reservations to get us a place to stay while in Vegas. By the time the summer of 2017 came along, we were feeling pretty good about things, and the trip was becoming about the only thing any of us could talk about. Lo and behold our first and only major snag was put in front of us.

Before the trip, Jason, Paul, and I went out to go find a geocache that hadn't been found in a very long time. I had already crossed it off my list, but the adventure to get to it was so incredible that I had wanted to go again. So off we went and made our way through the woods of Albert County up to a cache that most people in the region would never bother with. During the trek, Jason let Paul and I know that he was going to have to drop out of our trip. He didn't want to say a whole lot but basically said that he had some issues that needed to be resolved and that he couldn't take care of those if he went on the trip. I was disappointed as Jason is a fantastic guy, and I would have loved to have traveled with him, but I respected his decision and knew that he wouldn't have dropped out if it wasn't serious. We finished our geocaching for the day, and I went home and gave the news to Ken. This presented a new problem. Who could replace Jason?

For a short time, we considered going on the trip with just the three of us. Budget-wise, we could still afford it, but the cost per person was definitely a lot higher than we really wanted. That became the last resort option should we not find anyone we felt was compatible enough to do this trek with.

We threw around a couple of names of people we knew, but it was difficult to think of another individual that we thought would fit well with us for those two weeks. Between the three of us, we all knew a lot of people, but it was surprisingly hard to think of someone that would gel with us. We knew that whoever came with us had to be able to afford it, and could take time off, and be someone we'd be able to get along with during that entire time.

Ken and I had drinks with Ron and made a soft inquiry about if he was up to it. Although flattered by our request, he didn't think he would be up for such a long trek but wished us luck on our search for another traveler. Our other former PEI traveler really wasn't in a position to be able to join our crew at the time either, so the search continued. Then one of us made the suggestion to ask Mark Knowles if he wanted to come. We'd all known Mark for ages, and Mark was probably one of the friendliest guys you could ever meet. He was also someone I had met through geocaching but had come to know a bit more about him over the years. Mark was a businessman and someone who had done a lot of traveling on his own. He owned a limo company for a while and spent a lot of time driving down into the USA and back for some of his clients. I saw him more often after I became a freemason and joined Keith Lodge #23 in Moncton (a Masonic Lodge), and after he purchased the gas station down the street from my home. Always a guy willing to help out those in need, Mark is truly a genuine soul. It seemed like an almost obvious choice to ask him to join us so Ken and I decided that the next time we saw Mark, we'd ask him.

One night while out at the Masonic Club, I spotted Mark on the deck manning the BBQ and figured this was the chance to ask him about the trip. Ken had already asked me if I had hit Mark up yet, and I was literally on my way to go ask. I went outside, started up a conversation with him, and he actually asked about how the plans for the trip were going. I then told him about our predicament and asked if he wanted to come. He said he'd check with the boss (his wife) and let me know. Within a few days, he confirmed he'd be able to come with us, and that was it. Our replacement had been found.

We had created a Facebook group for all of us to share different ideas and updates on things we had in mind for the trip. Ken had actually posted a suggested update to our route that would allow us more time to see the Grand Canyon, and even get our Wyoming geocache a little earlier. It seemed like each day, another little tweak to our route got added.

During the long weekend in August, we ran a trial run of our "live tracking" software for our website. I had built the site in such a way that it would display every geocache found by any of the "4 Guys" while we were on the road. It would post links to the caches in a little widget window along the side in the order we had found them. You could even plot them out on a map. The live tracking feature was something that I had spent a lot of time on and thought that folks who were following our adventures would enjoy it. Plus, when the trip was all over, the plot on the map would actually show us exactly where we were on a Google Map. The maps you'll see in the pages that follow were created using the tracking data we collected along our journey.

I had purchased a subscription for an app called FollowMee, which ran in the background of my phone and sent an update signal at timed intervals. The live tracking code on our site would pull and log the location history, and then plot it on a Google Map. During our trial run, we went to Truro for a mega event and came back, and I was glad we had done the test as it showcased a massive bug in the tracking code. Thankfully I fixed it, and then all was ready. It was now just a matter of waiting for one more month.

With only a few weeks left, each day that went by became harder and harder to bear. All of us were essentially just putting the days in knowing full well we were just waiting for that Sunday to arrive. Thankfully when the long weekend came, a big yearly geocaching event took our minds off the trip. Ken, Paul, and I went down to Kouchibouguac National Park for their annual event and spent the day talking to geocachers. It ended up being the perfect means by which to distract ourselves from the fact that tomorrow was going to be the big day. By the time the event was over, we had plugged our trip and adventures with the attendees, and it was time to go home, pack, and get ready for tomorrow. Sunday, September 3rd, was finally here.

Now, had we picked any other day, we would have left Moncton early in the morning and started our way down to the USA, but for personal reasons, we couldn't leave until mid-afternoon. That was all on me. September 3rd is my son's birthday, and there was no way that I was going to miss it. I travel a lot for my job, and I have always made a point of making sure I am home for both of my kid's birthdays. It is important to them and to me, so I've kept my promise of staying close during those days. Both of my kids knew about my big trip, and I had made a deal with my son that his family gathering for his birthday would happen for lunchtime and that I would be leaving afterward. I had told Ken that as soon as I was ready, I would text him. He and Paul were going to go to Mark's place and wait as he lived literally around the corner from me.

My son had his party, blew out his candles, had his cake, and as happy as I was that he was turning 10 years old, I was more excited about getting on the road but tried my hardest to hold it in. But when he unwrapped his gifts, and the celebration was over, I knew I was ready to go. A quick text message to Ken and within a few minutes, the van pulled up in front of the house.

Since our logo had all four of us leaning out of a car, my wife got us to pose in the van in the same way. That shot was the first real image we posted to Instagram for our website. From that point forward, we were officially on the road. Well, almost.

The van was rented from Enterprise Rent a Car on West Main St in Moncton. Ken had picked the vehicle up before we could leave on our excursion, but we all had to stop at the rental office for them to make copies of our licenses. We didn't think it would take that long, but sure enough, after wanting to get on the road so badly, we stood there for what felt like an eternity waiting for the agent to finish with another customer before they took our licenses. It then felt like forever waiting for them to come back so we could leave. But eventually we did finish our visit there, got back in the van, turned right on to Main St, and the trip began. A year in the making, we were finally putting rubber to road.

Just Keep on Going

September 3rd, 2017

How a rush of adrenalin got us through the first 10 states with barely even blinking.

In the initial planning for the trip, we were supposed to drive from Moncton to around Portland Maine on Sunday and make Portland our official start of the tour early on Monday morning. The legs of the trip were broken up to have us drive for 14-18hrs per leg, take a 6hr sleep/rest break, and then repeat this again and again until we got to the west coast. This pattern would then repeat itself on our journey back home from the west. The intention was to give us bursts of travel time with decent sized breaks between them but also give us the ability to keep going more if we felt we didn't need the rest yet.

So when we hit the highway leaving Moncton, we didn't anticipate going much further than the middle of Maine. Knowing that the travel for the first day would be much less, we all knew that the first major stop for us would be the US border in Calais, Maine. We had decided to cross there and take the #9 highway, known locally as the airline road, because Google said it was faster. I had driven that road countless times when I lived in the US and traveled back home quite often.

To set the stage as to what it was like at the beginning, and for pretty much the entire trip itself, you really need to understand the four guys in the van. We're all middle-aged men, happily married with good jobs, jovial and off-beaten senses of humor, and generally all-around decent human beings. We're not really the jock type, although Paul plays a lot of hockey so he could probably kick all of our asses quickly enough. I'm a geek with my computer and science fiction obsessions. Ken's the talker, the whiskey drinker, and the outdoorsman, whereas Mark is very worldly, kind, but still has a badass sense of humor about him.

Understanding who we are as people will help you appreciate the kinds of conversations and topics that went on in the van as we were bouncing down the road. With four guys in a car and no women around, the jokes got a little dirtier. The comments got a lot more lewd. With no boss, spouse, or other individuals around, the sound and dialog in that van turned more and more into a raunchy teenage movie than anything. From conversations about the sizes and smells of our excrement to comments about the latest attractive looking celebrities, in many ways, it felt like being in the locker room of a football team after having won the championship. No topic was off-topic. It's best described by noting that within less than an hour of being on the road, the request to put MacLean & MacLean on the stereo came. I'd been listening to those two Canadian brothers tell crap and fart jokes for years after my good friend introduced me to them in high school. There was no better comedy troupe to put on the radio for the four of us as we drove through Saint John, New Brunswick.

In no time flat, we made our way up highway 1 heading towards St. Stephen. I had been posting updates on our Facebook page as well as my personal Facebook profile as we were traveling. Over the past few months, we had all really been spreading and pushing the news about this trip and that people could follow us and see what we were up to.

Eventually, we started to work our way up towards St. George, and we began to get a few messages from a couple of our geocaching friends. Audrey & Andrew were telling us to dig out our cameras and be ready to snap a photo as we went by a particular exit. We had known them for a long time as they had been active geocachers in our region. We weren't entirely sure what we were looking for, so as we got closer and closer to the exit, we just decided it would be easier to take the exit and see what the big deal was. As we approached, we could clearly see some kind of sign hanging over the edge of an overpass as we took the exit. We parked the car on the side of the road, got out, and walked over to find both of them holding a large sign that they had been hanging over the edge of the rail.

Instead of snapping the photo from the highway, we got them to give us the sign, and all four of us held onto it as they took a picture of us. A huge thanks was given to them as we shook their hands, posted the photo on social media, then hit the road again. This time Mark switched it up and got in the driver's seat as the next stop would be the border to the US.

In what felt like the blink of an eye, we popped into St. Stephen and made our way for the US border. Since we had already pulled the plug on the Canadian provinces on our route, this would be the only crossing going into the US. The real question was whether or not the customs agent would believe what we were doing and whether or not we'd be searched. At some point during the trip, Ken had mounted his GoPro camera to the dash to act as a dash-cam in case we saw anything unusual. The camera never did record anything of note, save for the actual crossing into the United States. We all dug out our passports as we pulled up to the border agent, took a deep breath, and then waited for the questions.

As someone who travels into the United States a lot for my job, I'm fairly used to dealing with the customs folks. Between my work visa and my other specialty customs documents, I have minimal issues crossing into the US, but I always still feel a bit of anxiety as if I am somehow going to end up in trouble just for wanting to visit the US. You hear horror stories in the media about people getting stuck at the border, searched, harassed, or questioned extensively, and it can fill your head with a bunch of preconceived notions about what happens. Even with all the crossings I do, I still wonder from time to time if this will be the one time I cross that they decide to give me a hard time. This instance was going to be a bit different as it's not very often a van crosses the US border telling the agent they are visiting every state over the next two weeks. The last time I had taken a long trip through the US by car, I was traveling alone and was questioned considerably by the agents, had my vehicle searched extensively, brought into the office and questioned more, and even got instructed to go back to the Canadian side to get specialty paperwork. I was hoping this time it would be a different story.

Mark was fantastic at explaining to the customs agent precisely what we were doing. The best way to describe the reaction of the agent was to say that there was a long pause after Mark told him we were doing all 48 states in two weeks. The silence was long enough that we all noticed, and it was clear that the agent was processing in his head whether or not we were lying. He asked about what kind of GPS units we were using, and we showed him the ones we had. I remember clearly sitting in the van with my heart pumping on overtime, wondering what else we would have to explain to him before we'd be allowed to enter.

Just as I was starting to think there might be an issue, the agent then grinned and asked who the horse was. We had purchased a set of two magnetic mats, each about the size of a mousepad, which we clung to either side of the van. The image depicted was our "4 Guys In A Car" logo, which had Ken shown as a horse since he was always wearing his horse mask to various outings. The moment the agent asked about the horse, we all smiled and breathed a huge sigh of relief. We chuckled, and Ken chimed in and told him he was the horse. The agent then wished us luck and waved us through. The biggest hurdle of getting into the US was over. Within 20 minutes, we made a pit stop at the Irving just at the start of the #9 highway before making our way down to Bangor. But not before snagging our first official geocache of the trip and getting the first state sign.

It had been decided early on that we would do our best to stop along the highway and take a photo of each state sign as we crossed the border. Snagging Maine was relatively straightforward as the roads around that area had plenty of places to pull off and park. This would not be the case for several of the other state signs we would get later on in the trip. Further down the road as we headed towards the Irving Station, we spotted a cache on our map and decided to get it. Even though all four of us had already found caches in this state, we had decided to find at least two caches in each state we visited regardless of our personal find history. By finding at least two, it guaranteed that if one of them happened to be deleted by the geocache owner for some reason, we'd still have the other one as a backup. I popped out of the car, and one of the guys snapped a photo of me grabbing a cache from a guardrail. After that, the airline road was next.

In 1999 I spent a year living in New York State. During that year, I made several trips back home and always took the airline road when I returned. Having done that trip so many times, I knew the route to and from Poughkeepsie New York, as well as I know my way to work in the morning. I also knew that the worst part of the trip, in either direction, was always getting through the state of Maine. Maine isn't a large state, but it's also not a very small state either. When you travel north or south from one end to the other, it feels like an eternity of looking at nothing but trees for 5 hours. Sitting in the car, seeing nothing all that noteworthy for all that time, could make that portion of the trek quite dull. The road itself is a two-way highway, so when you get stuck behind someone, it can feel like forever as you wait to get a passing lane and go by them finally. It took a full two hours to get to Bangor, which would become another pit stop for us. We needed to eat, and for both Ken and me, we wanted to pick up a US sim card for our cell phones so we could use the data access without getting huge fees from back home.

We popped into an AT&T store and picked up the cards we needed then headed over to Five Guys to have supper. Talk about the best burgers and fries around. I have since been back to other Five Guys spots around the US, Canada, and overseas and I can tell you, they do not disappoint. By the time we got out of there, the rain had come, and we knew we were trying to get to Portland for the night. I had booked a Hilton for us to stay at, and then we would continue on our trip after a 6-hour break at the hotel.

The rain was coming down hard, and we started getting closer and closer to the hotel, and none of us were tired or really all that interested in stopping. We knew that we had a lot of distance to cover, but we also knew that we needed to take time to rest and sleep as we needed. Even though our original plans had us staying the night, we started talking about whether or not it made sense just to keep driving. Mark made the suggestion that we mainly just keep going until we hit Chicago, then crash there for the night and get a full, good night's sleep. We could then repeat this same pattern for the rest of the trip. For the most part, we'd drive straight through for about a day and a half, roughly 36-40hrs straight, then crash for a good 8hrs or so. By driving straight through, we'd save time on the travel, which we could then use to help us get a good night's sleep every second day. Everyone in the van seemed to think this made sense, so we opted to skip the hotel entirely and just keep on trucking.

Looking back now, I can tell you that this was a game-changer for that trip. Originally the schedule for our legs was designed to have us stop a lot more often but have 4-6hr "breaks" where we would either sleep or just rest and relax as we needed to. We'd designed the route that way so that we could still cover all of the territory we needed, but get more breaks. Going straight through for 36 hours or so would be a lot more tiring for some of us, but then being able to get a bed and a good night's sleep in a hotel would vastly improve how we felt overall. There were times where we did have relatively long stretches without sleep, and we certainly felt it, but changing it up like this severely helped us get to our destinations much faster and with a lot better rest between.

I called the Hilton, and after being bounced around on the phone a bit, I got the reservation canceled but had to forfeit the points I had used to make it which was a bit disappointing but was then quickly brushed aside as I now knew our next real stop was going to be in Chicago. We would need to cover 1800kms by the next night and snag close to 20 geocaches across nine different states. Losing some frequent stay points was well worth the changes to our plans.

When we hit New Hampshire, we knew we couldn't take the standard interstate highways to get where we needed to go. The route we had plotted had us cutting across New England through portions of New Hampshire and Vermont. Once we went past Portsmouth, NH, we got on the 101 and headed west towards Vermont. Now the thing about not taking the interstates is that you take a hit on how fast you can drive, and depending on where you are, the roads can be pretty terrible. We followed the 101 to Manchester, and eventually, it led to the 202, which took us directly into Vermont. At this point, it was pretty late. In fact, I think it was safe to say that we were pushing towards midnight, possibly into the early morning.

Regardless of what time it was, the places we were going through were dead. The sun had long gone down and any caches we were snagging we were now doing in the dark. We'd pull over to the side of the road, go find a cache with our flashlights on, get back in the car, and continue along. At some point during our winding-road excursion through small-town Vermont, Ken decided to get into the backseat and start drinking. Somewhere around Bangor, we had made a quick detour to pick up some snack food and drinks. It was during that stop that Ken picked up a couple of alcoholic beverages for him to enjoy later. We all knew he wouldn't be driving anytime soon and was likely to get some sleep anyway, so we didn't think much of it. That was until we came to a stop at a red light in small-town Vermont.

With Ken in the back with a bottle of whiskey in his hand, I was sitting in the front seat on the passenger side. As I look out the window, lo and behold, it's the police station. The van had stopped directly in front of the local sheriff's department, and here we were with a guy drinking with open alcohol in our car. When the light turned green, we moved along and made sure that if we did get stopped by the cops, Ken would take the blame for being the one drinking in the car. Not that it mattered as his indulgence tapered off long before we hit Chicago and rarely surfaced again during the trip. At some point before hitting New York State, we managed to grab a few geocaches in Vermont to include that state on our journey westward.

After having spent about 5 hours or so traveling through the state of Maine, it was nice being able to knock out a few more states in a short time. I had printed a list of all 48 states we would be visiting in the order that our route had us traveling. Each time we would get a new state, I'd dig out the sheet of paper and cross off one more. By the time we finally did get to New York State, the sun had started to come up, and the veil of night was finally lifted. As lovely as it was to have daylight again, New York State would serve as the first of several prolonged states to drive through.

See, the thing about New York is that when you hear of New York, the average person thinks of New York City and doesn't give much thought about the state itself. Having lived in Poughkeepsie (pronounced puh-kip-see) New York for a year, I heard plenty of folks complain about how the rest of the world only sees NYC and not the state itself. If you look at the state of New York on a map, it's kind of shaped like how your thumb and forefinger look when you make a "gun" sign with your hand. For us, we were traveling from about the edge of the thumb all the way to the other side of the index finger. That's a little over six hours of driving just to get out of one state. Although that seems like a long time to be in one state, we would learn later on in the trip that traveling across this was nothing compared to some of the others.

Not long after snapping the photo of the state sign that read "New York, State of Opportunity" (as opposed to "The Empire State" which you see almost everywhere else), the first city we were looking for was Albany. The town itself wasn't all that meaningful to us, but it served as yet another milestone on the map. On any journey that covers as much territory as this one did, any major city we passed through felt like a bit of a minor accomplishment moving us closer to our primary goal. We knew that driving through this state was going to be a long one, so first it was Albany, then Syracuse, Rochester, and then Buffalo. Driving by the home of the Sabres, we knew that we'd finally reached the end of the main cities within this state and that Ohio would be coming up soon.

Like most long road trips, there were times where the

conversation and jokes in the van would go on for quite a while. But then you would get these long stretches of silence where everyone in the van is just tired, and thinking about where we were going and what was coming. When I wasn't chatting with the boys, or posting something online for folks back home, I was either trying to catch a few blinks of sleep here and there or just sat there staring out the window. At this stage of the trip, there was so much more excitement about the whole thing than there would be during the return portion of the journey. Gazing out the window, watching the trees and buildings zoom by, I started to smile as I thought to myself that when this was all done, I'd have a great story to tell.

In no time flat, the van began to see signs for Cleveland, a city I had come to despise over the years. Since my career had started taking me on the road, I had visited Cleveland far too often. Known as the city that rocks, you would think that it would be a place people would enjoy. Being downtown during a business trip, and as someone who doesn't really do bars, or go to sporting events, there wasn't much for me. Even the Rock & Roll Hall of Fame seemed pretty lame the one time I went as it had three whole floors dedicated to The Grateful Dead. I'm sure there are plenty of people who love the city and swear by how great it is, but for me, I was glad for us to drive through and not make a stop. Oddly enough, I do have a clear memory of passing through there on this trip as we all spotted a massive cloud of smoke that seemed to be coming from an airfield. We never did find out what happened, but we all wondered if there had been some kind of aerial accident that sparked the fire.

We blew through Cleveland and passed by Toledo and made our way to Michigan. Even though we were trying to get at least two geocaches in every state, we knew that, in some cases, that might not be possible. Michigan was a state that we wondered whether or not we would be able to get more than one cache since we really were just taking an exit, getting a cache, and then heading back out on the highway. But the geocaching gods were good to us that day and provided us a bit of luck.

Geocaching has a lot of different "types" of geocaches. The most common type is a traditional geocache, which is a physical container located at a specific set of GPS coordinates. But there's also something called a "virtual" geocache, which still has a set of coordinates for you to find something, but there's no physical container. In most cases, there is some kind of statue, plaque, or other landmark that the hider wants to bring you to, but a container can't be placed for various reasons. In Michigan, this was the "Tristate Marker" geocache, as depicted here. The marker was placed in the middle of the road and actually  represented the border between Michigan, Indiana, and Ohio. This would be the first of many unique and memorable locations that geocaching would bring us on this trip. From that spot, we acquired a cache for Indiana and two for Michigan, all within about 200 meters of the virtual itself.

But getting through those states was another milestone on the trip as we started to see the light at the end of the tunnel for this leg. Illinois was coming up soon, and Chicago was going to be our final major destination before getting our first good night's sleep. Zigzagging out of the middle of nowhere, we hit the highway again, made one minor detour to snag another cache for Indiana, then crossed the border into Illinois and pointed ourselves at Chicago.

Chicago was another city I had been to several times, and I knew that the best place for us to go would be downtown to Millennium Park to visit the bean.

Officially known as the "Cloud Gate", the bean is a giant monument located in the park shaped like an actual bean except for the fact that the entire surface of the monument is made of a bent reflective material that allows you to see your reflection. This location was yet another virtual cache and would become the most notable geocache location of the first leg of our trip.

I navigated us downtown while Mark found us a place to park. We got out of the van, walked up a set of stairs, and then came outside to the sound of traffic and the sights of tall buildings everywhere. Aside from making quick stops for the things we needed along our trek, this was actually the first real extended stop on our journey. Coming up from the underground parking and seeing the park and buildings all around us, it was a really nice change of scenery and pace for us as we knew we could take a few extra minutes to really enjoy where we were.

After having dialed in the location of the bean into our

phones, we crossed the street and made our way to the park. As always, it was filled with countless other people taking photos, and the four of us were no different. The photo depicted here shows all four of us staring into the bean as we all took pictures of our reflection to mark our arrival into Chicago.

But for us, the plan was never to stay in the windy city itself but to go get the bean virtual cache and then find one other geocache and continue on our way. Although we had planned to travel west from Chicago, we did have one more state that was just north of Illinois that we had to snag before moving on. We could have easily waited and grabbed it in the morning, but given that Wisconsin was not that far from Chicago, it made a lot more sense for us to just suck it up for a bit longer and grab the caches in that state before calling it a night.

After doing the bean, we wandered over to Buckingham Fountain (as seen from the TV show "Married With Children") and got another cache there. All in all, we probably only spent about an hour downtown before heading back to the van and pointing ourselves north. By this time, it was pushing towards 7 pm, and we knew we needed two caches in Wisconsin. The drive would be about an hour, so by the time we got there, snagged our caches then turned around; it was getting a bit late. Pleasant Prairie Wisconsin ended up

being just what we needed as it resides just shortly after the border, and we were able to find a couple of caches relatively quickly before heading back towards Chicago.

We intended to head back down towards the I-88, hang a right onto the highway, and then pick the first hotel/motel we could find on the western outskirts of Chicago. As we continued to drive along the road, Ken did some Google searches and made some reservations for us at a little motel, and eventually, we did finally make our stop in Naperville, Illinois. The cost of a room was relatively cheap, especially when it was split between all of us, so Ken had booked two rooms. We checked in, got to our rooms, and found ourselves more than happy to put our heads down on a pillow.

That first leg blew by so quickly that we didn't even realize how tired we were, but the magnitude of what we had already accomplished didn't escape anyone. We'd driven from Moncton to Chicago straight in less than two days. The total amount of travel time was somewhere in the vicinity of 32 hours or so. Mark's suggestion to drive through the night and get a good sleep every second day was a complete and total time saver for all of us. But even more important was the fact that we'd get to have a real sleep, on a real bed, and actually take a real break before pushing ahead again.

Ironically, when I finally did get into my room and into bed, I wasn't tired or ready for sleep. I turned on my laptop and watched a little TV before the fatigue really hit me. When it did, I was out cold in a flash. Thankfully I knew that I'd get a full night's rest before getting up and taking on leg #2.

Are We There Yet?

September 5th, 2017

Long stretches of little to see with eyes on getting as far as the Pacific Northwest.

The first full leg of the trip was over. We all got up in the morning, had a quick bite to eat, and then hit the road. Everyone knew that this particular leg of the trip was going to be a long one, but none of us realized how long it would actually be. I had made the mistake of turning off the GPS tracking app on my phone when I went to sleep the night before, so for the first two hours of highway driving, no new points got dropped on the map, which you can barely see from the image shown. It's a bit funny to look at the map now and see this very noticeable gap between Naperville and Joslin. Thankfully I turned it back on and never shut it off again the entire trip.

If our actual destination had just been Washington State, we would have merely traveled west out of Illinois and headed directly north up towards the Dakota's and then made our way to the Pacific. But since we needed to get all 48 states, we had to make a minor southern detour once we hit Des Moines Iowa. We'd have to travel south through Missouri down towards St. Joseph Kansas, then pull a full U-Turn and head north.

A meal stop along the highway found us grabbing some KFC but not before I got my own little surprise while visiting the men's room. Sitting on the can, minding my own business, I was playing on my phone when I turned my head upwards to find a man standing there looking into the stall. I was startled and quickly asked the guy what the hell he was doing. It turns out he was the maintenance man and just wanted to make sure the stall was clear. I promptly told the man I was okay and to mind his own business. I pulled my pants up and got the hell out of there as fast as I could.

Driving through Iowa and Missouri, we found the landscape to be riddled with farms filled with corn and dust. Cruising along, I looked out the window and saw the endless fields and was reminded of a similar experience from 20 years prior. I had taken a road trip from Moncton to Los Angeles in 1997 and had driven through much of the same areas we would be traveling this time around. While sitting in the van, it was like a little flashback remembering the dark clouds rolling in and wondering if the movie Twister was going to play out on the highway. I smiled, looked at the guys in the car, and was immediately reminded of how lonely it was to be driving all that way by myself. This time around, it was undoubtedly a whole lot better to be in the company of good friends.

Rest stops were few and far between, and much to our delight, we discovered that "ding dongs" are a real treat you can buy at the gas stations here and were not something we had back home. The only memorable thing we spotted on the highway was an Oscar Meyer wiener car driving on the opposite end of the freeway. You can't imagine how unorthodox it is to be driving down the interstate at 75mph and spotting a giant hotdog coming in the other direction. We all chuckled, and I grabbed my notepad and wrote it down.

The first cache we found in Missouri was this little rest stop in the middle of a farmer's field. There were these flat metal sculptures made to look like various animals, including bulls. Having had very little to entertain us during our drive through this part of the country, Ken and Paul posed for what I can honestly say is one of the most hilarious photos we took during this entire trip. The 15-year-old kid in me laughs every time I see this.

When we finally made it down towards St. Joseph, Ken wanted to get a sim card for his tablet so he could use it for navigation and other things that required internet access. We pulled into an AT&T shop at one of the exits just before crossing the Missouri River into Kansas and waited. And waited. And waited. I am sure we sat in the van waiting for Ken to get his card for almost an hour. At that time, I found myself having to answer the call of nature, so I took to crossing the street to head over to the gas station to find some relief. Two gas stations side by side, and neither of them had a bathroom I could use, so I had to hold it until better facilities would become available. I got back to the van, and Ken was still waiting to get his card done. Finally, he emerged from the store, tablet in hand, and then proceeded to tell us about the complete lack of service in the store.

We had picked this area precisely because we knew we could cross the bridge into Kansas, snag a few caches, then head north on the I-29 and make our way to the Dakota's. The view across the bridge was quite lovely, and we ended up snagging a cache just off some side road that gave us an even better view of the river. We opted to take the long, or I should say the more scenic view of returning back to the main highway via some back road near the airport. The road was in serious disrepair, and the van was bumping and bopping in the dirt, but we eventually popped back out onto the highway and continued on our way as the sun started to go down.

Driving along the I-29, the state of Nebraska was just on the other side of the river. We kept a close eye on where geocaches could be found. We knew we could easily pick up a few caches while traveling through Omaha, but knowing it was getting darker, we wanted to try and get the caches taken care of before nightfall. It's not like we really cared whether or not we would be caching at night as we'd done enough of that already, but we knew we had a long haul of driving come up and wanted to get some of these smaller states out of the way.

Exit 10 came along, and we noticed two caches relatively close to the Nebraska border and only a couple of minutes from us, so we took the turnoff and hung a left heading towards the Lewis &

Clark Interpretive Trails. But before we got to the trailhead, we spotted an unexpected familiar vehicle parked in a no-name parking lot off the main road.

We pulled into the parking lot of an antique store/coffee shop and spotted the Ecto-1 from Ghostbusters. Here we were in the middle of Farmville nowhere and one of the most famous hearses of all time was just sitting there. A few of us got out and snapped some photos of the replica of the movie vehicle, laughed at the oddity of seeing it in such an unusual place, then got back into the van to make our way to the caches.

The view of the river from the trailhead was quite nice, but for us, it was all about getting the two caches on that main trail and snapping a photo of the state sign. Throughout this trip, there were very few opportunities for us to do much hiking. But this happened to be one spot that we did get a chance to go for a walk in the woods to find a few caches. I remember walking along, thinking about the fact that the sun was going down, and it was so quiet compared to the chatter and radio in the van. By the time we got back on the highway and headed towards Omaha, the veil of night was coming down, and we knew we still had a full 24hrs of driving left.

On a trip like this, there are entire sections of the journey that are far harder to recall simply because nothing notable happened. From Omaha to Fargo, we crossed through Iowa and South Dakota, captured our needed two caches per state, stopped when we needed to stretch the legs, and just found ourselves doing what needed to be done more than anything. As it always is, you fill a van with four middle-aged guys who are bored stiff, conversations about sex, drugs, alcohol, men's parts vs. women's parts, television, movies, each of our abilities to snore loud enough to be heard in other states, and anything else that comes to mind would always seem to pass the time. We'd often switch the radio to something local, then one of us would play some of our own music from our phones, then other times we'd just have silence in the car, and the folks in the back tried to catch a few zzz's.

When we finally hit Fargo North Dakota, it was another milestone for us as it would be the final stop on our northern journey through the US on this leg of the trip. Due to its location, Fargo made it easy for us to capture two states instead of just one. We crossed the state line into Minnesota and drove around some empty parking lots in an industrial area, trying to find a few caches there. At one point, we spotted some rabbits running around the parking lots of some of the local businesses. That seemed to be about the most interesting thing we had seen since the Ecto-1. After snagging the caches, we turned westward, got what we needed from North Dakota, and then began the long haul across the northern US.

I don't think any of the guys on this trip would argue with the fact that the haul from Fargo to Yellowstone National Park felt like it was the longest of the journey. Driving across North Dakota alone took more than five hours to complete. The corn we'd seen in farm fields would be replaced by countless cattle and would be the only notable wildlife we'd seen on that entire stretch.

The only other memorable thing about driving through North Dakota was a very brief stop in a place called Dickinson. I didn't remember the name of the town until I looked up the GPS coordinates of a photo I took when we stopped there. It was the sign I spotted in the parking lot that prompted me to get the guys to pull the van off so I could take a photograph of a restaurant I had been poking fun at for many years. I was utterly blown away by the fact this place was actually real.

As a massive fan of the television show South Park, I had counted the season seven episode Grey Dawn as one of my all-time favorites. In the episode, senior citizens in South Park are causing a series of automobile accidents around the town and eventually have their licenses revoked due to the repeated injuries and deaths associated with their driving. The center of the joke is the fact that every one of them is trying to make it to "Country Kitchen Buffet" which is an early-bird diner in the town where all the seniors eat.

I had been making jokes about people trying to get to

"Country Kitchen Buffet" for years after that episode came out. When I spotted this giant sign that said "Country Kitchen Restaurant", it was the closest I was ever going to get to the same thing in South Park. I told the guys we had to stop and take a photo. We didn't stay for the food and kept on trucking, but it was a nice little stop in an otherwise dull haul through North Dakota.

One thing about North Dakota was that in some places, the land just seemed to go on and on forever. In the photo taken here, you can see an excellent panoramic view from a rest stop near Hailstone Creek just as the sun was starting to come up. There may not have been a lot to see in the farmlands of the Dakota's but looking out here and seeing such a beautiful view, it was easy to see how some would want to come here just to escape from the busy rush of the big city.

Getting across Montana, dipping into Wyoming to get Yellowstone, to make our way to Spokane Washington was 11+ hours. But before that could even begin, we had to finish our trek through North Dakota which had already gone on too long.

When morning rolled around on September 6th, and we finally spotted the Montana state sign along the side of the road, we were all quite delighted to finally be in a new state. At the time, we had no idea that Montana itself was going to feel like the longest of all the states we would drive through. Even though California would rival it to some extent, Montana seemed to have a whole lot less for us to see.

Our first and only major stop in all of that state would be a small town called Wibaux.

It was early in the morning, and no one was to be seen anywhere. In some ways, the town reminded me of "Puente Antiguo" from the movie Thor. One major road seemed to travel "downtown" with not much else to be seen in the area. We did manage to find a cache located at an old stone-built church that had been in the town for centuries. The multi-colored stone of the building really made it stand out. We snagged that geocache and two more in the same little village before heading back out on I-94 heading towards Bozeman.

In the course of driving across all 48 of the contiguous states, some states we would pass through and barely have any memory of. Other states would stand out as milestones because of experiences we had there or specific sites we got to encounter while on the road. Montana was different in that it stands out as feeling like the longest of all of the driving we did. At just under 11 hours, it was a state that just seemed to keep going and going and never looking to end. It was also a state that had a stark contrast from one side to the other. In some spots, it felt like an endless sea of farmland, but as we got closer to the west side, the farms were replaced by an almost desert-like terrain.

Taken at a rest stop near Hathaway, Montana, this photo shows a little glimpse of the Yellowstone River far before we would ever hit the national park of the same name. In fact, Wyoming was a bit of a difficult task to try and figure out exactly how to incorporate it into our route.

Our original plan for the western portion of the US had us traveling to Wyoming during our return trip back to Moncton. We had planned to drive upwards from Las Vegas to Salt Lake City and then up into Wyoming and across the I-80, then coming down through Denver. This would have made for a really nice drive through Utah, Wyoming, and Colorado. But during the month before our departure, Ken had come up with a plan to be able to snag Wyoming on our way westward, trimming off a bit of time on our return trip home. Although I would have liked to have gone through Salt Lake City, it made a lot more sense to merely "dip" into Wyoming to get the caches we needed. But that too presented another unique problem.

The original route had us traveling across the entire state, which gave us all kinds of geocaches we could find both on and off the highway. When we switched the route to dip into the state from Montana, there was a noticeable geocache problem. As soon as you cross the border into Wyoming just after Gardiner Montana, there are no geocaches present anywhere. The only ones that are listed are inside of Yellowstone National Park, and all of those are non-physical geocaches.

Most of the time, when you go out and find a geocache, you are finding a physical container that has been hidden somewhere. There are various "types" of physical caches, but they all share the characteristic of having a physical box or container of some kind that you have to find, open up, sign your name, and re-hide back where you found. Physical geocaches are prohibited from being hidden in many of the national parks within the United States. So to attract geocachers to these places, non-physical geocaches have been "hidden" in place of ones with a physical container. These geocaches bring you to a specific location and have you either take a photo of yourself there or answer questions about where you are to prove that you actually "found" the place.

The act of "finding" the location or container goes hand in hand with what geocachers refer to as "logging the cache". This is merely the act of writing a log message on the geocaching website for the specific geocache you have found. By logging it there, your profile gets updated to say you have found it, your find count gets increased, your geocaching statistics are updated based on the nature of what you found, and the owner of the cache you logged receives an email notification that someone has found their cache.

Since there's no actual log to sign within a container for non-physical caches, when a geocacher logs one of these through the website, it's up to the owner of the listing to decide as to whether or not the log is considered valid and let it remain. Logs on non-physical caches are only permitted if the person who found it has satisfied the requirements set forth by the owner in the listing. The owner can delete the found log, and the finder would be without that particular find on their stats. We knew we needed to make sure that we took extra precautions to get these caches right so that our logs would be allowed. Most of the time, it isn't an issue, but some virtual geocache owners have been known to be very particular about what they want to see in their photos or answers received. It's this very same reason we had chosen to get at least two geocaches in every state. If one of our logs were deleted, we would still have at least one other find for that state.

When we finally did get to Gardiner and made the turn south to hit Yellowstone, it was nice to get a bit of relief from the state of Montana. Just outside the border of the park, we pulled off to the side of the road and got out. Ken had been admiring the river since we started to see it as we got closer to the park, so when we had the chance, we pulled over, and Ken asked us to take a photo of him standing in the river. Ken is a hunter and fisherman, so his love of the outdoors was really showing when we landed here.

The drive into the park was quite scenic, and we were fortunate to spot some elk, bighorn sheep, deer, buffalo, mule deer, and even a few cows all while exploring the little bit of the park we got to see. That in itself was a bit of a disappointment in that we really only had enough time to find what we needed for our trip before we would take off. The park also reminded me that as much as I like to keep my temper at bay, every once in a while, it does slip out.

We'd been up all night and had spent all that time in Montana, so for whatever reasons, my patience was wearing thin. Ken's well known for his colorful and sarcastic commentary from time to time, and we had heard and laughed at plenty of it while on the road. But when Mark opted to park the van in a spot other than one that was about 100m closer to where we were heading, Ken made some comment about being too far from the cache as he opened the door and walked out towards the visitor's center. I wasn't entirely sure if it was just a joke or another one of his comments, but I barked out a handful of colorful, not so flattering words in his direction. Somewhat stunned, Paul turned around and looked at me with a face that asked: "Are you ok?!?!" Reacting to his expression, I realized how tired and cranky I had become. I took a moment to collect myself before I got out of the car and followed Ken and the others to the store.

The first couple of non-physical caches we came upon asked a series of questions that were a lot harder to answer than we had initially thought. We did manage to get a cache located in a sort of unmarked graveyard just off the beaten path in the park. At the time, that would serve as the only geocache we would get for the state. Even though it was just the one, we knew it would have to do as the clock was ticking, and we needed to keep moving. Turns out later, Paul was able to log one of the other caches with the information he had, so that eventually did give us the two caches we wanted for that state. Once we had completed what we needed at the graveyard, we made our way back to the car. We knew we had to get as far west as we could before calling it a night. One way or the other, we had to be in Seattle by 2:00 pm on Thursday, September 7th. It was the only appointment we had on our calendar for the entire trip that we had to be at for a specific date and time.

For us to visit the headquarters of geocaching located in

Seattle, you had to make an appointment or risk not being able to visit that day. So we booked it at that time, knowing we had to push ourselves. At mid-afternoon on the 6th, we really wanted to try and get into Washington State that night so we could make our way to Seattle in the morning.

After we got back on the main highway heading west towards Idaho, we started to spot smoke in the distance. As night began to fall and we got closer and closer to the Idaho border, the smoke actually became more and more prominent and in some spots could easily be smelt. A few Google searches later, it turns out that Washington State had some severe forest fires, and it was the smoke from those fires we were seeing.

As it got darker and darker and night came upon us, I remember keeping a close eye on the Google map just anxiously waiting to cross that state line into Idaho. It was a state we wouldn't be in for very long as the northern tip of the state is very narrow, but after having gone across Montana for about 11hrs, when we spotted that blue sign coming up on the highway, it felt monumental and that we could just take a moment to breathe and be glad we had finally gotten out of Montana. It also helped all of us push, knowing that Washington State was not that far ahead of us and that a good night's sleep would follow soon enough.

Driving through Idaho at night meant that we weren't going to see a whole lot. What I do recall of that drive was that the roads seemed to weave in and out of the woods, and no matter how hard I tried, I kept wondering if some kind of animal was going to pop out and get in our path. Paul was driving, and we were both getting pretty tired and just wanted to push through and get to the next state. We had set our sights on Spokane Washington, as it was right near the border and would only be about a three and a half-hour drive from our first stop the next morning.

Crossing the border into Washington State wasn't anything dramatic in terms of what we saw but in its own way, was a fantastic accomplishment. It was Wednesday night, and we had left Moncton on Sunday afternoon and were now crossing into the most western state 3,000+ miles later. Such a short period had passed by, yet we had already crossed the entire country, and tomorrow, we would hit three major geocaching milestones, plus start our southern journey down towards California.

Eventually, we came through Spokane and started looking for a place to crash for the night. We purposely drove through the city and came out on the western side so that when we left in the morning, we'd already be on our way out of the city. By the time we got into the motel room, it was pushing towards midnight, and we were exhausted, but more than happy to have traveled all that distance in such a short period. We wouldn't be claiming a full 8hrs of sleep this time, but as soon as we hit our pillows, we were all out cold.

From Milestones to Giants

> September 7th, 2017
>
> Three geocaching milestones, a view of San Francisco, some tall trees and the lights of Vegas

September 7th was going to be the most significant geocaching milestone for this trip. Although the reason behind the journey was to snag all 48 states in one excursion, it was this day that gave us three major geocaching attractions in a single day: The APE cache, Groundspeak Headquarters, and the Stash Plaque.

With more than three million active geocaches across 191 countries, there are plenty to be found. But some of those cache types are very rare and therefore sought out by geocachers who want to have that type of find in their stats. The "APE" cache comes from the official geocache type "Project A.P.E.". From the official description:

> *"In 2001, fourteen geocaches were placed in conjunction with 20th Century Fox to support the movie Planet of the Apes. Each geocache represented a fictional story in which scientists revealed an Alternative Primate Evolution (A.P.E.). These geocaches were made using specially marked ammo containers and contained an original prop from the movie"*.

When we first started planning our trip, there was only one APE cache in the world, and it was located in Brazil. A couple of weeks before we left on our trip, the APE cache hidden in Washington state was re-activated, making it available to all geocachers. So for the four of us, being able to get the APE cache while on this trip was a huge bonus. We would then follow up getting the Groundspeak HQ cache (home of the official geocaching.com website. More on that later.) after visiting the offices later that day. But for now, we had to get to the "tunnel" as quickly as possible, so we could get the cache and be on our way to make our appointment at 2 pm.

After leaving the motel and driving for several hours, we took exit 54 off the I-90 West and headed into a parking lot that served as the trailhead to Snoqualmie Pass. From there, we would hike a total of about 10km round trip through the Snoqualmie Tunnel. This was an abandoned train tunnel that ran through the Cascade Mountain range in Washington State. The famous APE cache was located just past the west side of the tunnel. I had found the APE cache several years prior, but the tunnel had been closed for maintenance, so I never had the chance to go through it. Being able to hike the tunnel was pretty exciting. But before we could set out on our journey, I had to make a phone call.

Between all of us, we had been posting things about our journey on our website, Instagram, and Facebook and the local newspaper caught wind of it. I got asked to do an interview with Times-Transcript about our trip. I called the reporter from the van and spent about half an hour chatting about our excursion so far, and what we were doing, what we had seen, and why we were doing something like this. We'd get back home and see our photo in the paper, along with an excellent article about our journey. With the call over, now it was time to hike the tunnel.

We paused to take a photo before we hit the tunnel, but even there we could feel the cold air. It wasn't that cold outside, but since the tunnel itself was closed off to the outside elements, there was nothing in there to keep the temperature up. The brisk air surprised us as we entered, and before we knew it, the light from the entrance to the tunnel was gone, and we were amid a pitch-black abyss.

Have you ever walked through a tunnel where no light gets through? The only thing we could see was the light generated by our headlamps, as well as a tiny spec of white that appeared far off into the distance. At first, we thought it was an actual lamp or some kind of light inside the tunnel, but as we got closer and closer, we realized that it was the light coming from the other side of the tunnel that we had seen from so far back.

The walk itself was relatively easy. It curved from one side to the other, so it wasn't just a flat straight line from start to finish. You get about a mile in, and the light from the entrance is no longer visible because of the curve. Although it was relatively dry in there, there were spots where bits of water had seeped in, and you could definitely see  your breath as you walked. It was a lot colder than I expected but still remained a relatively easy hike to get through with no change in elevation. Before we knew it, the actual light at the end of the tunnel came into focus and more visible. We popped out the other side and took a moment to soak in what we had just done.

The actual APE geocache was only about 400m or so from the tunnel, but our time was starting to tick. We knew we had to try and get this done as quickly as possible, as getting back to Seattle on time was incredibly important, and it was at least an hour's drive to get there from the trailhead.

We found the giant tree and rock pile where the APE cache was hidden, signed our names, took some photos, then turned back to make our way again through the tunnel. There was another geocache that was located along the trail that was considered to be one of the oldest active geocaches in the world. We wanted to try and find it but knew there was only a limited amount of time. Paul took a small detour on the way back to the tunnel to snag the cache for us, and then we met up at the opening to the tunnel. Before we knew it, we had popped out the other side and were back on the highway heading to Seattle. An hour later, we found ourselves downtown trying to find a place to park near HQ.

Groundspeak is the name of the company that runs the main geocaching.com website. It's not really fair to say that they invented geocaching as that really came from a guy named Dave Ulmer. But Jeremy Irish and the original founders of the geocaching website can really be credited with allowing the hobby to grow and become what it is today. Their headquarters is located in Seattle and can be visited by anyone by making an appointment. The act of visiting the location allows you to log a find on a particular "HQ" geocache, which is its own type in your list of finds. I had been to HQ once before, but it was in a different location, so despite having already "found" it, it was new for me as well.

We finally found a parking spot and were quite amused by the means for which you pay for your parking. Most parking lots have a machine you simply swipe your credit card through, and it spits out a ticket which you place in your windshield to prove you paid for your parking. This lot had no such machine. Instead, we were presented with some kind of metal panel attached to a post and a sign that said to "Pay Here". The panel had a series of squares, each with a number and a little slot about 2" wide and maybe .5" high. The numbers corresponded to the parking spots in the lot.

Scratching our heads at how we were supposed to pay the vague directions finally clued us in. We needed to fold our cash payment and slide it into the slot for the spot we were parked in. I chuckled in amusement as the parking meters were all electronic, yet this parking lot needed you to literally stuff cash into a box to pay for their services. With our money now "shoved" into our slot, we crossed the street and headed upstairs to see what HQ was all about.

We got off the elevator on the 3rd floor and walked into HQ to find what you would see at a gift shop but with a bit more of a geocaching theme. One wall (shown in photo) had a pile of unique swag only available to visitors to HQ. Greeted by a young man, he welcomed us and gave us the low down on what there was to see and experience. On one side of the office was a giant treasure chest, which was the "geocache" for this location. It was filled with a ton of goodies, including trackable items that could be taken and dropped off.

Wait, what do you mean by "trackable items"?

Within geocaching, there's actually an entire sub-culture around "trackable items". Groundspeak issues special "trackable codes" that can then be placed on virtually any kind of object but are mostly seen on what is known as "travel bugs" or "geocoins". Once registered on the website, a geocacher can drop the trackable into a geocache then mark that it has been left there. Someone else can then retrieve it and move it to another geocache. This repeats again and again as the item "travels" the world. Using the unique code, you can look up where the thing has traveled to. Trackable items have been known to collect tens of thousands of miles as they visit around the world, and the online map shows their exact progress.

Many geocachers love the idea of sending these out into the world to see where they end up. Ultimately, most trackable items go missing as people mistake them for things they can trade in a geocache versus a trackable item. Like travel bugs, geocoins also have the unique code on them but are actual minted coins with a unique design. These are often made for special occasions, events, and challenge programs. For us, we collected a few trackables from HQ and dropped off a few ourselves before checking out the rest of the office.

A photo booth was along the back wall, and we were told to go in and take some photos. Two copies of the photo strips would print, and one of them was for you to keep, and one was to be placed in one of the logbooks sitting on the table. If you knew of someone else who was going to visit HQ, you could tell them to try and find you in one of the books.

Lucky for us, we also got some free geocaching trackable items, including one specific for HQ and a few others that were in limited availability. All four of us picked up some unique swag, including trackable geocoins, a hoodie, and a bunch of other little stuff that we knew would make great souvenirs of our visit. I even gave the receptionist some geocoins from back home and thanked him for his time. Back outside, we wanted to try and go see the "troll" before hitting the road again.

Seen here with Paul, the Freemont Troll is a famous

landmark located under the north end of the George Washington Memorial Bridge in the Freemont district of Seattle. Another spot I had visited before but told the boys we had to go see it. There was a geocache located in the same area, but despite our efforts, we were unable to find it. Instead of spending too much time finding a single cache, we wanted to hit the road as we knew we were likely to hit afternoon traffic on our way out of the city.

Alas, we were too late and ended up stuck in heavy traffic on our way out of town. It was sometime around 4ish when we had finally got back on the road, and it seemed to take forever to get out of the city. The intent was to try and get to Portland before nightfall because our last major geocaching milestone was going to be a big one, and we would have preferred to see it in the daytime. Just over three hours later, we'd take a couple of crazy turns down a long and windy road and then stop at this significant milestone of geocaching lore. But to understand what it meant, you need to know a bit of the history and origins of geocaching and GPS technology in general.

Before the spring of 2000, any non-government or non-military GPS unit was subject to something called "selective availability". This "feature" introduced random errors into the GPS accuracy causing consumer units to only be accurate to within 100-200 meters or so. As a result, even though GPS technology was available since the 1980s, it was virtually useless to consumers unless you were privy to a unit that could suppress the selective availability. Military or government-issued devices had a means for offsetting this feature and were as accurate as our modern-day GPS devices to some degree. On May 2nd, 2000, the US government permanently disabled selective availability, and all GPS devices worldwide suddenly could pinpoint a location within 10 feet or so. This act is what gave birth to location-based services such as Google Maps, Uber, and countless location-based games like Pokémon Go. But before any of those were even a thought, GPS technology spawned the first location-based hobby: geocaching.

On May 3rd, 2000, a man by the name of Dave Ulmer hid a container in the woods near Beavercreek Oregon just outside of Portland and posted the GPS coordinates on a Usenet group called "sci.geo.satellite-nav" and told folks about what he had hidden and wanted to see if anyone else could find it. He called it the "Great American GPS Stash Hunt". Within a couple of days, replies came up saying they had found his container, and now others wanted to do the same. This was how the geocaching hobby began.

The original hide placed by Dave is now long gone, but a plaque was placed with permission in the spot where the first container was hidden. Known as the "Original Stash Plaque" (GCGV0P), it has become a bit of a legend for geocachers. For us, it can be somewhat of a pilgrimage from all over the world to be able to get here and log the find where it all began. There actually is a physical container to sign just behind the plaque.

Finding the stash plaque would complete what is known in geocaching as the geocaching triad: The APE Cache, Geocaching Headquarters, and the Stash Plaque. We really wanted to get there and see it in the daytime, but it wasn't in the cards.

For us, we pulled the car just off the road after driving down this long and weirdly shaped winding road and spotted the plaque. We all got out, took a bunch of photos, and found the actual nearby container.

There was another cache very close to the original, and we knew we needed two caches for the state, so it was an easy decision to snag both. All four of us with flashlights out were searching in the middle of the woods for this little container. Again, for myself, I had found both caches in a previous trip but could not for the life of me remember where the other one was, so I was wandering around aimlessly like everyone else. We did eventually find it, sign our names, and then headed back out on the road. Our next major stop was going to be San Francisco.

Just before we got on the highway near Portland, we made a pit stop at a convenience store to pick up some drinks and snacks for the road. It was in this store that we all encountered that part of the United States that we had heard about, but hadn't yet seen on this trip.

Generalizations about an entire country can be incredibly inaccurate because you can't take a country with a population of 300+ million people and say they're all a certain way because that's simply not the reality. But as a Canadian looking into the US, I can tell you that generally, I have seen two kinds of American people.

The first kind of Americans are very similar to many Canadians. Friendly, easy to get along with, interested in caring for each other, and seemingly normalized to some degree. I have many colleagues who live and work in the US, and culturally, I would not see them as being any different than anyone I know back home. For me, almost all of the American people I have met or dealt with would fall into this category. The woman standing behind the counter at the convenience store would fall very clearly into something else.

We all went up to the counter to pay for our stuff. I made some comment about the fact that I found American money confusing because all the bills are the same color, and as a Canadian, I'm not used to having single dollar bills. That one-off comment lead to what felt like a harmless conversation with the store clerk. This was all well and good until she handed me my change, and I made a comment about the fact that Canadians don't have pennies.

The clerk got into a big uproar about this and started to go off on how you can't let the government take things like your pennies away from you. She went on about how it starts with something as simple as pennies, and then eventually they'll take away your rights to own a gun, and then your children's rights to go to school, and that the government has no business taking anything from you. She seemed absolutely convinced that because we had made the decision to get rid of what really is a useless piece of currency, it would be the downfall of our entire country.

All four of us sort of stood there insanely surprised by this reaction. I don't recall what I said, but it was something to the effect that getting rid of pennies was never going to take away my kids' education, and I walked out of the store repulsed by the ridiculousness of her ideas.

Everyone is entitled to an opinion, but it really struck a chord with me as it showed me a side of the American people I had rarely seen. Every now and then, I encounter folks from the US whose ideas about government and personal rights just seem so disconnected from the mindset of many other Americans. I'd love to be able to say that the current political climate within the US is to blame for this, but I'd seen this kind of distrust of government long before the current president ever took over.

Sadly, this one experience now stands out as the only memorable, non-geocaching experience I have had in Portland, Oregon, and more so, that entire trip. There were very few instances during those two weeks where I spoke to or interacted with the locals and felt like the mindset was so completely irrational. Thankfully, I was able to get my stuff, go back to the van, and prepare for a long drive to San Francisco.

To get from where we were outside Portland to the bay area was going to be about 10+ hours. This would compare timewise to how much time we spent driving across the state of Montana, yet for this stretch, for some reason, it didn't seem to drag on as much.

The Caravan Chronicles

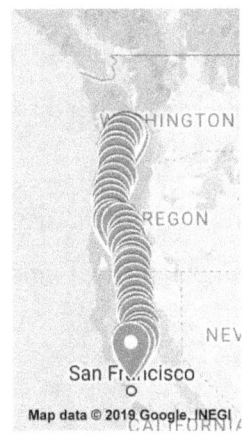

You can see from our tracking map that we made almost a straight line from Portland to San Francisco, but a large portion of that travel was done in the middle of the night.

Paul recently told me about how he had gone back through some of our routes and punched up Google Street View to see some parts of the highway and course that we only really saw at night. It turns out there's all kinds of things we drove right past and had no idea even existed because we were trying to get from one specific location to another in the middle of the night. It's probably the only downside to this kind of trip is that there were plenty of things to observe along the journey that we'd have to skip simply because of what we were trying to accomplish.

Around 3:19 am in the morning, we crossed into California, and then just before 7:00 am we stopped for a bit of a break at a rest stop about an hour north of Sacramento. The only reason I remember stopping is seeing the crawfish wandering around the parking lot, snapping at cars and people's feet. I had never seen one before and thought they looked like little lobsters walking on the sidewalk. You could poke at them, but they'd come after you, so I instead I snapped a few photographs and moved on. We only had a couple more hours before we'd hit San Francisco and take a break from driving.

Initially, when the route for this trip was planned, we had intended to make Seattle, Las Vegas, and New York, the main cities that we wanted to visit while traveling. But almost as soon as we started plotting a route, both Jason & Paul had suggested taking some time to see San Francisco as it was a unique place and would serve as a nice break along the way. The intention was to spend a few hours in the city seeing a few sights then heading west towards Las Vegas. With Sacramento now behind us, San Fran was next, and we had to decide how we'd approach the city.

If you punch in Sacramento to San Francisco into most navigation apps, it won't have you cross the Golden Gate Bridge. Instead, it has you take the I-80 to bring you downtown. Our original route actually did not have us crossing the famous bridge, but as we got closer to the city, we opted to shift our course so we could get a shot at seeing an icon of the area. On a trip like this, you needed to take advantage of seeing any major iconic landmark along the route, even if it meant taking a bit longer to get where you were going.

Just before crossing the bridge, we opted to park the car at the Golden Gate Bridge Vista Point and go for a walk to see the view. I had been to San Francisco a few times but had never been to this part of the bridge before. We actually went under the bridge as we walked over to the park and got what would typically be a fantastic view of the bridge and the river. But much like many other tourists, we got stuck with fog on the river that morning and could only see a portion of the bridge in the mist. For us, it didn't matter a whole lot as we took in as much as we could see from that one vantage point. Also fortunately for us was the fact that we were able to snag our first California geocache right there in the park.

With some photos taken, a Facebook live stream broadcasted, and a geocache snagged, it was time to get the rest of what we wanted out of the city taken care of. Part of our plan was to spend a few hours checking out Fisherman's Wharf, Lombard St, and seeing if we would have any luck spotting the bushman.

A quick Google search of "San Francisco bushman" will yield a ton of videos and a Wikipedia article about a man by the name of David Johnson, who is known as the World-Famous Bushman. I had heard the story of this guy while I was working for Whitehill Technologies. A colleague told the story of how he was walking along Fisherman's Wharf in San Francisco when a man, who was crouched behind a bush, jumped out and scared him. It turns out this is Mr. Johnson, as mentioned earlier, who busks as the "bushman". I had forgotten the story when I was there on business and went for a walk and was startled when he jumped out at me. I laughed and then recalled the story I had been told. When we made plans to come here for our trip, I told the boys we'd have to try and go see him.

It was around 1:00 pm when we started wandering around the wharf going in and out of some of the shops, taking photos of the streetcars, spotting ships in the bay, and just enjoying the atmosphere of being out of the car and somewhere actually enjoyable beyond geocaching. We had been up all night and still had a ton of driving and other things to see, but the break from the road was much appreciated. The bushman was nowhere to be found, but oddly enough, we did actually find his bush with some belongings locked to a fence, so we knew he was around just not in the area at the moment.

For geocaching, we snagged a virtual geocache at a place called Sal's, which was mostly an old arcade museum. There was a ton of old pinball, arcade, and other amusement machines located within this one building. We had to solve a puzzle given in the listing by going around the entire museum looking for specific items to answer a question. Another geocache we found involved getting our photo taken on a webcam right on the marina itself. You can see all four of us in the picture towards the bottom right with Alcatraz in the background.

Doing the webcam geocache allowed us to see something we hadn't expected. If you looked out into the water from some spots along the docks, you'd occasionally see the odd sea lion swimming around. But when we got to the webcam, it was clear why the camera had been set up and why there were so many people. An entire portion of the dock had been taken over by sea lions. They were sitting up on the pier itself, all kicking back, having a snooze with a few of them making enough racket to be heard all over. I'm sure we must have stood there for quite a while, just taking in the wildlife and enjoying being there on the docks.

Another famous spot in San Francisco we opted to try out was the famous Lombard Street. Most of the street itself is pretty straightforward, but it's most notorious block is the one that has eight hairpin turns on it. It's one giant zig-zag that goes downhill, and for those who have a larger vehicle, good luck. As we drove down going left to right and back, there were a few spots where we noticed that people actually had driveways on that road. I couldn't for the life of me imagine trying to get out of a driveway there. For us, just getting the chance to drive it in our rental van as part of our exploration of the city was enough to mark San Francisco as a notable stop along our journey.

After having lunch, Ken picking up a sailor's captain's hat, one more geocache in the area, and it was time to move on. What we didn't know at the time was had we remained in the Bay Area longer, we may have caught the folks at Marvel shooting a movie. Ant-Man & the Wasp was shooting in San Francisco during the week we were there. A few days after we had left there, I'd get wind of this via a Twitter feed I follow that shows filming locations. That would have been a cool extra to add to the trip, but all things considered, San Francisco was a nice touch for us.

But the last major thing about San Francisco was that we

marked it as really the last of our southern journey. We had one more stop that was still in California, but it was more east than the south, and the real end-game now for us was to get to Vegas with one major stop in between.

I didn't talk about it while I was on the trip, and I don't think I've ever really said too much about it to anyone before or after, but there was something else about taking this trip that was important to me. I knew going from one end of the country to the other would mean we'd hit a lot of places that I had been to already either for work or vacation. But even with all of the travel I had done over the years, it was rare that I ever got a chance to share any of these exciting places with my good friends back home. For this trip, I was as excited about being able to share with my friends some of these amazing places I had been to before, as well as just enjoying the experiences that went along with this particular journey. So despite the fact I had done the geocaching triad or been to the Bay Area before, I was excited for a much different reason than they may have been.

Now that being said, it was actually Paul who made the suggestion about our last stop on our California journey to a place that I didn't know much about; The Sequoia National Park. He'd been asked by someone he knew if we would be anywhere near it. When he looked up what was there, he was flabbergasted by what the park contained and then conveyed that to the rest of us who immediately made sure it would be included in our trip.

This national park is known mainly for the incredibly large and tall sequoia trees. Five of the most towering trees in the world live within this park, including General Sherman, who is the largest known living single stem tree in the world at the height of 275' and a diameter of 25'. In 2006, the largest branch of the tree broke off and destroyed a portion of the perimeter fence and cratered the pavement of the surrounding walkway. That alone tells you about how massive and powerful these trees really are. Many of the trees in this forest are so large or tall that no description of them or even a photograph does them justice.

The journey to the park started with us having to make our way to Fresno, California. We knew that it would be somewhere between four and five hours to get to the park so we needed to make sure we got there before sunset otherwise we wouldn't see any trees at all, and it would have been a wasted trip as going to the park was a real detour from the major thoroughfares that would get us to Vegas faster.

When we finally hit Fresno, we took the 180 east highway headed towards the park, and eventually, after about 45 minutes or so, we entered the edge of the park and started the very entertaining journey to the big trees themselves. What made the trip so funny? It provided Paul, Mark, and I an opportunity to see a side of Ken we never anticipated.

The park itself undergoes a radical change as you move deeper and deeper into it. Of course, you start to see the trees as you get more into the heart of the park, but it's actually the elevation change that you notice before you ever see any of the big guys. I don't recall the exact starting elevation when we entered the park, but according to Wikipedia, the lower elevations are right around 1,700'. This looks about right as we went into the park we would notice the signs that would indicate a change in elevation. At one point, the elevation we reached was as high as 9,000'.

Driving along the "Generals Highway", all you really get to see is a bigass forest as your vehicle weaves in and out of the trees along a very narrow road. If you drop a Google Street View marker on the road near Buena Vista Peak and start moving along in either direction, you can get an even clearer picture of how narrow the lanes are and how there is no guard rail to speak of anywhere along the way.

At first, when you're at a lower altitude, the lack of protection from the side of the hill doesn't seem like such a big deal. It looks pretty thick with trees, and it's not that far of a drop to down below. But the further you weave into the middle of the park, the higher up you get and every once in a while, a viewpoint will come out and remind you of exactly how high you really are.

According to the GPS altimeter, this photo of Paul catching a glimpse of the park was taken somewhere near 5,000'. As we continued through, this number would continue to grow and grow as would the amount of anxiety Ken would have sitting in the back seat.

We'd all known Ken for a long time, and one thing I can say is that in as long as we had known him, Ken was never really overly anxious, nervous, or even scared. But when it came to Mark's driving through this zig-zag climb through the mountains, to put it bluntly, Ken was losing it sitting in the backseat. As Mark would come around a corner, Ken's knuckles would turn white as he squeezed the overhead handle all the while telling Mark to slow down and not to get so close to the edge. He'd be frantically looking in and out of both windows wondering if we were going to go over the edge. Paul and I commented on the fact that we'd never seen him so nervous, and he would say he was fine, but then make more anxious comments about the drive through the hills. At the time, we kept trying to calm him down, but thinking about it now, I'm pretty sure that the entire drive and seeing him freak out like that was one of the most entertaining things about that day.

Eventually, we started to see the trees. One could be spotted from the van, and we'd stop the car and have to pull our jaws up off the ground in shock of the sheer size. But then we'd turn our head and see another even bigger one. Each time we stopped the car, this same pattern emerged. You couldn't fathom that any of the trees would get any more prominent, and yet each time we spotted another one, it was, in fact, larger than the last.

Sunlight hours were becoming less and less, and we knew that the biggest of the trees we wanted to see were still on the horizon, so we buckled down and opted to skip any further stops. Mark did his best to speed his way to the trailhead near General Sherman but with the road as it was, and Ken losing his mind in the backseat, it was a slow and arduous drive to get there. Eventually, we did get to the trailhead, even after driving by it and having to turn around, parked the car, and made our way to General Sherman.

The photo of all four of us at the base of this tree is nice enough, but unfortunately, it does not really illustrate the sheer size of the tree in contrast to us, especially where the top of the tree is not visible from this angle. I managed to snap a series of different photographs that show various views of the tree from the bottom upward, but I still struggled to find the right perspective to give a sense of the size and scale of these trees.

It's the sheer magnitude of how big these trees are that it is incredibly challenging to showcase through written word or even a photograph. Digging through the countless photos I have of this area, none of them provide any real sense of the grandeur of what we saw and experienced in that forest. Although not depicted here, there were several trees where the base of the tree was actually opened, and you could stand inside the trunk with room to move around on any side. I took a handful of vertical shots trying to show myself in comparison to the trees, but they were simply so large that no lens on any camera we had was ever going to be able to prove it. We spent less than an hour exploring that little area and the enormous trees that engulfed all of us, but eventually, time took over, and we needed to make our way out of the park.

Having spent that entire time going up to get to the trees, it also meant that we would have to do the reverse in going down the mountain to get out. Despite it being around 100km distance on that road from start to finish, it takes about two hours to drive it because of the motorway itself and the speed limit. Since it was the end of the day, and there was construction on the main road out of the park, the time to get back onto the main highway and on our way was far more than it should have been. The construction on the road caused one lane of the road to be closed for a portion of the drive. Add to that, because the sun had gone down and the streets are so twisted, we had to drive incredibly slow to make sure we got out of there alive. On more than one occasion, a car from behind us would cut into the other lane and illegally pass us only to get stuck behind another vehicle that wasn't too far off in the distance.

Looking back at the map and seeing the road after the trailhead, it's pretty clear that there was a whole lot more twisting and turning on that end of the road than there was on the side we came in on. I think it would have been even more entertaining with Ken had we come in from that side. Not being able to see the edges of the road or the drop in the dark made it far less nerve-wracking for Ken on our way out.

Eventually, we did make it out and headed towards

Bakersfield, where we could get back on a major highway and hit I-15 towards Nevada. By the time we hit the interstate, we had been up for around 37 or 38 hours, with a whole lot of activity having filled that time. It would have been effortless to simply just get a motel in Bakersfield and call it a night, but Mark had booked his room in Vegas for a Friday night check-in which meant that if we pushed through, we could check into a real hotel and then finally be at our halfway point.

Mark did the driving on the last portion of this leg as we came into the state of Nevada. I'd been to Vegas a few times, but Mark was an old pro at the area and had spent a considerable amount of time in Vegas itself as well as the surrounding states. I was in the passenger seat while Ken & Paul were half asleep in the back. Mark and I chatted about travel in general, as well as Nevada and Las Vegas. He made a comment about how you could easily spot the border between California and Nevada purely by the lights. As we got closer to the state line, he was spot on as the glow from the casinos and hotels right along the border stood out like a sore thumb. We snapped a photo of the state welcome sign and knew that we'd be at the hotel in less than an hour.

Most visitors coming into Las Vegas arrive via air at McCarran Airport and then typically make their way to a hotel down on the strip. With us coming in via I-15, we got a chance to see the south end of the strip in the middle of the night.

First, it was the Las Vegas South Outlet shops, which we

very quickly breezed by. Then in a snap, we could spot the airport on our right with a couple of helicopter pads visible from the highway. As we drove by, I wondered if we could spot any of the "Janet" airplanes that are used to shuttle staff to and from Area 51. But then just as we were coming up near the Luxor and Mandalay Bay, Mark took a side road, and we skipped the next part of the strip entirely in favor of just getting where we needed to be.

We pulled into the Polo Towers parking lot, and Mark went off to get us checked in. I remember sitting on a couch waiting for him and wondering how much longer it would take before I could put my head down to get some sleep. We finally got checked in and were out cold in no time flat. It was just past 3:00 am on Saturday morning, and after having driven all that distance in just a week, we finally would have a chance to take a breath and enjoy a few days of stress-free visiting before hitting the road again on Monday.

No Time Like Our Own

September 9th, 2017

Sin City provided us the perfect place to take a pause from all the driving.

The fact that none of us had to get up at a particular time on Saturday morning meant that we all had the most stress-free sleep we had had in a week. There was no driving required. There was no next stop we had to get to. No appointment had to be made. It was the first and really only time during that trip that there were no obligations to meet, and we could just relax and recoup some energy from the insanity that had been the last week.

At best estimate, we would have covered in the vicinity of 9,500kms at this point, all with only three major stops for sleep in Chicago, Spokane, and now Las Vegas. The most significant portion of our trip had already been accomplished, and in fact, as of the night before, we had pointed the van in an easterly direction on our return trip home. But before we'd even consider getting back on the road, it was time for a break.

When initially planning the route, Las Vegas was always the halfway point. For both Mark and I, we had access to pretty decent accommodations there at a ridiculously low rate, so it made a lot of sense for us to just use Las Vegas as a spot where we would not have to worry about anything other than recuperating from the intense drive. It may have seemed like Las Vegas would be the last place you would go to relax, given the lively nature of the city. But for us, it was a welcome change of pace.

Saturday morning, we woke up and wandered over to the Miracle Mile Shops, which were located directly across the street from the Polo Towers, where we had stayed for the night. After snagging some food at Blondie's, the trek along the strip began. Neither Ken nor Paul had ever been to Las Vegas, so the intention for that day was to try and see some of the more notable spots along the strip. Heading south along Las Vegas Blvd, we walked along the east side of the strip heading towards the MGM Grand. Snapping the odd photo here and there, I was enjoying that we had no agenda, and our time was merely our own.

By the time we got to the Excalibur hotel, we had taken the tram from there to Mandalay Bay and wandered our way back from there. I had forgotten that both Mandalay Bay and the Luxor hotels are connected through a little shopping area in the back. As we were checking out the casino and the shops in the mall, we spotted a small sports shop, and Ken wanted to pop in and check it out. Ken is a huge New York Jets fan and wanted to see if the shop had anything Jets related. Just as we were walking in, we noticed this little table off to the left-hand side, and sure enough, Pete Rose was sitting there giving autographs and photos.

Ken bought a baseball, which gave him the chance to get a picture taken. We asked him politely if we could all get a photo taken, and he said sure. It was an unexpected surprise. I'm not a baseball fan, but even I knew who Pete Rose was, so this was definitely cool.

A few photos of the Luxor hotel later, we were on our way back to the strip, and Ken made the suggestion that we try to have lunch at the "secret pizza" restaurant. I had never heard of it, but there was apparently a New York City-style pizzeria shop hidden somewhere in one of the hotels along the strip. There's no visible signage, and unless you know it's there, you will walk right by it having no idea there's food back there.

A handful of Google searches later, we made our way to the Aria Hotel and then eventually into the Cosmopolitan, where a friendly security guard told us where we could find the restaurant. Up to the third floor and to the left of Jaleo, we spotted this very narrow, unmarked hallway, and sure enough at the end of it, there was a little pizza place just waiting for us. The food wasn't anything spectacular, but the little adventure in finding this gem was entertaining.

A bit more exploring later, we opted to head back to the hotel and get changed as we had an event to attend to later in the afternoon. Since this was supposed to be a geocaching trip, we had listed a geocaching event at the Panda Express restaurant in the Miracle Mile shops. The event was set to start at 4 pm, and we didn't know who or if anyone would actually show up, but we figured it was an excellent way to meet some of the local geocachers. But before hitting up the event, I had to move my stuff from the Polo Towers to another hotel.

I had booked a suite at the Elara hotel as our accommodations for our time in Las Vegas. In the original timeline we had plotted, we were supposed to get into Vegas around noon on Saturday, but instead, we actually arrived late Friday night. Mark had already booked a room for himself for Friday-Monday, so when we rolled into Vegas at 3 am we just went straight to his hotel. I had already paid for mine, so I wanted to make sure I made use of it. Since both Mark and I had rooms with two bedrooms, Paul ended up staying in Mark's room while Ken and I moved our stuff over to the Elara.

I had booked the largest room my points would allow me to book as I figured all four of us would be staying there. In the reservation, it was listed as a 2 bedroom suite. I just thought it would be a room comparable to Mark's with only two small rooms. After going up to the 50th floor and walking to the end of the hallway, nothing could have prepared me for what was on the other side of the door.

In 13 years of traveling for business, I have stayed in a lot of hotel rooms. I've seen some pretty nice rooms, but I had never seen anything like this place before. The photo shown here is taken from the front window looking back towards the door. This was the "living area" but you can kind of see part of the "bar" in the kitchen near the back on the left. The first, small bedroom and bath was just behind and to the right of the table with the white chairs (there was a short hallway that connected them). The master bedroom was just to the right of the couch and had a full wrap-around view of the Strip, with a full whirlpool tub, standing shower, and full bathroom.

There were windows from floor to ceiling, and on one portion of the room, the windows were tinted red, which gave this fascinating tint to the city. Later on that weekend, I did some research and found that the daily rate for that room was somewhere in the vicinity of $2,500/day. For me, I had paid my $75 booking fee to use some of my specialty Hilton points, and that was it. I never did find out exactly how I ended up with that room but whoever opted to give it to me instead of a regular room, thank you.

Picking our jaws up off the floor, we dropped our stuff and then made our way downstairs and into the mall for our event. It was time to meet some local geocachers. Or so we thought.

As it turns out, we had more visitors to Las Vegas than locals coming to our event. Folks from Germany and England and a few from the US all popped in to say hello. We used a US $1 bill as our log for the event which everyone signed, gave out some coins, shared a few stories about our trip so far, and then wrapped it up. A quick hop across the street and into the car, all four of us made our way down to one of the most famous Las Vegas landmarks.

Along with creating a website and Facebook page, we'd had a few other things made up to promote the trip. At our event, all four of us wore our "4 Guys in a Car" t-shirts. After parking the car, all four of us got out and made our way to the famous Las Vegas Sign at the far south end of the strip and had someone take a photo of us standing there. Unfortunately for us, that night happened to be a night where some of the lights in the sign happened to be burnt out, but we didn't care — making it here marked another milestone for us along our big journey.

The plan was to head out from there, drop the car off, and take a bus downtown to Freemont Street to see the light show. We got to the pickup point near the Miracle Mile shops and were waiting for the bus when Ken opted to head back to the hotel. He had really wanted to come with us, but whether it was something he ate or just pure exhaustion, his stomach was definitely not feeling well and opted to steer himself towards the hotel bathroom instead of the sounds and lights of Freemont Street.

The bus ride was a welcome departure from driving, but I think we were more worried about trying to find a parking spot downtown than anything else. In retrospect, parking at Freemont Street is actually pretty easy as there's a decent-sized garage right beside the SlotZilla attraction. But at the time, it seemed we just wanted to let someone else deal with getting us to and from downtown.

Now, if you've never spent any time in Las Vegas, you may not know that what is commonly referred to as "the strip" is technically not in Las Vegas at all. Years ago, many casinos were built outside of the actual Las Vegas city limits to prevent the casino owners from having to pay municipal and city taxes. At one point, the city of Las Vegas tried to annex the property known as the strip to force the casinos to pay additional taxes. The casinos successfully lobbied to have that land designated as unincorporated townships such as Paradise, Winchester, and Spring Valley. This prevented the city from claiming that land and allowed the strip casino owners to avoid having to pay the city of Las Vegas taxes.

Freemont Street is part of downtown Las Vegas or "old" Vegas. The most notable portion of this area is known as the Freemont Street experience and runs from the Plaza Hotel & Casino to Las Vegas Blvd. The street itself continues east past the container park and to other areas as well, but most people associate Freemont Street with the sound and light show found on the western end of the street.

This five-block stretch of road is closed to traffic and is an open shopping, casino, and entertainment area. The most notable attraction of this section is the barrel vault canopy, which runs for four blocks at the height of 90' up. The canopy is essentially one giant LED screen that runs a light show. Every hour on the hour, the lights of the shops and casinos along the covered portion of Freemont Street turn off, and music is played in sync with the "show" being displayed on the canopy. The show itself is different every time and serves as the biggest draw for tourists.

Light show aside, there's also a zip line called SlotZilla, which runs from one end of the canopy to the other. Three outdoor stages feature concerts from various artists typically given for free by the city. The world-famous Heart Attack Grill can be found here where patrons wear hospital garb and are served by "nurses" who will paddle you if you don't finish your entire meal.

But along with the sights and sounds, you'll find plenty of street performers. Dancers, musicians, and spray can artists litter the entire area just waiting for folks to watch and tip them for their show. On weekends, this whole section serves as really one colossal party that draws massive crowds. Paul, Mark, and I did the walkthrough from one end to the other several times to just soak in everything there was to see.

We must have stayed downtown for a couple of hours just enjoying the light show, the pretty girls in showgirl costumes, and the music blasted from the stages. For Mark and me, we had both been to this part of the city several times before, but for Paul, it was all brand new. I found myself just wanting to play tour guide and show all of the coolest parts of this section of the city for Paul to see. I felt bad that Ken didn't get a chance to enjoy it with us, but after hearing the stories of how he felt once he hit the hotel room, I was glad he opted to stay back. Eventually, we got back on the bus and headed back to our hotel rooms to crash for the night.

The following morning we were set to head out to Hoover Dam and snag a few caches along the way. But before hitting the highway, we made a quick little stop in a parking lot on the south end of the strip. It turns out there was another geocaching event that was happening that morning for some folks visiting from Hawaii. We made an appearance and met up with a few people who had come to our event the day before. Met a few other cachers and shared stories of where we had been and what our plans were. After exchanging pleasantries, we got in the car and pointed it east towards Hoover Dam.

To get to Hoover Dam from Vegas, you can simply follow the I-515 and I-11 and go there directly. We decided to take a little detour and follow highway 93 through Boulder City to find a couple of virtual geocaches. It wasn't that far out of the way and made for a nice little detour. There was no time limit or schedule we had to follow for the day, so taking some extra time to soak in a bit more of the state of Nevada was fine by all of us.

One thing that many may not realize is that the desert itself has its own unique beauty. I've been in several different desert-like terrains around the world, and every one of them has always offered up an impressive view of the landscape. When someone says desert, you tend to think of giant sand dunes with people wandering from dune to dune looking for water and wondering if they are going to survive. Except for one specific trip, all the deserts I have visited over the years are nowhere near the look and feel of Tatooine from Star Wars.

This photo was taken from the side of the roadway where we stopped at for a geocache in Boulder City. I took the panoramic shot from here because I thought it was actually quite beautiful in its own way. Although there's still green bushes and vegetation everywhere, you can clearly see how dry and desert-like the terrain really is. With the mountains in the background and Lake Meade barely visible, it still makes for a sweet scenic spot even though there's not much life to be seen here.

We eventually left Boulder City and made our way to the dam, which was less than a half-hour away. We opted to drive past the dam first to the end of a scenic highway, which Mark had told us was the better route to take. Kingman Wash Access Rd led us to a really nice lookout point, but not before we made a quick stop at the little gift shop. The only reason I remember the shop was that it was the first time I had ever seen US one-dollar bills used as souvenirs. They had actual legal tender $1 bills that had different pictures on them. From The Big Bang Theory to Pokémon to Star Wars characters, I was fascinated by the altered currency and picked up a few to take back home. Ken grabbed a penny wallet to hold the flattened penny collection he had started while on the trip. You take a penny and two quarters and put them into a machine, which then presses an image onto the penny as a souvenir. They're a cheap little keepsake but still a lovely memento of wherever they happen to be available.

Atop of the lookout point, we got a pretty good look at Lake Meade. Ultimately we made our way down to the actual dam itself and took a bit of time taking in all of the views. I'd been here before with my wife on a tour we had taken while in Vegas for vacation, but our time there was extremely limited. This time I got to see a lot more of the dam itself and some of the ancillary spots around it.

After wandering around for a while, we got a stranger to snap this photo to mark another milestone for us. We also took a bit of time to make sure we had snapped a couple of pictures of both the state signs as well as the actual divider that shows where Arizona and Nevada meet.

Not long after taking this picture, but just before we stopped to get the details on a virtual geocache at the dam, Paul had crossed the street and took out a water bottle to perform a little science experiment. He told me about how he had heard that if you pour a water bottle off the dam, the water will actually blow straight up. But when he cracked his water bottle open, poured it off the side of the dam, down it went. Whether it was the wind, the heat, or just something that day, there was no magical water flying up towards us.

After snagging the virtual geocache, it was time to head back to Vegas. The drive back to sin city was uneventful, but as we narrowed in on getting back into town, we pondered what to do to fill the time. How we ended up at a custom car shop is something I would never have expected, but to get why we ended up there was really because of Paul.

All four of us are pretty well-rounded individuals, but if you want to slot us into categories, then I was considered the geek, Ken was the smartass, Mark was the business-man, and Paul is the car guy. Paul's worked in sales in the automotive industry for years and even did some racing in his day. I knew he obviously was well versed in cars as he sells them, but I had no idea he was interested or even followed any kind of custom car work. He had made the suggestion that we check out a place called "Count's Kustoms" which is an automotive restoration and customization shop based in

Las Vegas. It's owned and operated by Danny Koker, who was a recurring character on the reality show Pawn Stars (for which we did drive by at one point). The shop is featured in the reality show "Counting Cars" and Paul thought it would be cool to go check it out. I'm about as far from cars as you can get but Paul had been so quiet about places he wanted to see that when he mentioned this place, it was a no brainer to go check it out.

Just off Westwood Drive and onto Presidio Avenue, we took a turn and eventually found our way into the parking lot where we were greeted and shown where to enter. Paul knew the area immediately from what he had seen on TV, and as soon as we entered the building, it was clear this place was all about some serious cars.

As a kid, I had a picture of a Lamborghini Countach hanging on my wall. I loved the look of the car but had never seen one up close. Walking into the main showroom of the warehouse, a white one was parked just beyond the velvet rope, and for just a minute or two, that young kid in me smiled and remembered what it was like to want a seriously cool car.

The showroom itself was a decent enough size to show off a dozen or so different cars along with a little gift shop. You could quickly tell how giddy Paul was by the amount of swag he bought and brought home. We explored a bit more and then hit the van and drove up to the end of South Highland Drive to check out another car garage featured on another show.

The show "Vegas Rat Rods" is shot at a shop called "Welder Up". This place was a completely different experience from the previous garage. Whereas the prior was all about restoration and more customization of vehicles, this shop was more about taking an automobile to an entirely different level.

These weren't about restoration and were all about showcasing an automobile art form. In the picture shown here, the motor is depicted with roses growing out of the main engine block with several other creative changes made to the vehicle to give it that spark of life that was utterly unique. It was a smaller shop, but the custom work we got to check out here was pretty spectacular and made for a great little stop along our Vegas tour.

Since this was going to be our last regular day in Vegas and neither Paul or Ken had seen the other side of the strip, we parked the car to do a bit of exploring down towards the Mirage hotel. We had spotted a White Castle restaurant directly across the street and wanted to snag some food, so we popped in, ordered, sat for what felt like an eternity, had some food, and then did some more exploring. From the Venetian to the Palazzo, we did the circuit up to the corner of Treasure Island and the Wynn hotels. You may not realize it, but a big part of exploring Las Vegas is going in and out of the big hotels. Each hotel has some kind of significant attraction that draws people in. From elaborate shows to fountains or gondolas, there's always something interesting to see in these places. We made our way south down the strip, passing Caesars and the Bellagio until we eventually hit the Shake Shack near the New York-New York hotel where we had our final meal for the night.

Much like New York City, if you spend any time in and around the Las Vegas strip, you'll find that before you know it, you've been walking for several miles. The distance from the Fashion Show Mall to the Mandalay Bay alone is about 5kms (3 miles), and we had walked more than half of that distance in just that day alone but also went in and out of the various hotels and attractions. If you ever visit Las Vegas, bring a good pair of walking shoes as you will definitely need them. For us, by the time we had chowed down some food for supper, we were tired, so we called it a night and went back to the hotels to settle in for the evening. Or so the other boys would believe.

On every trip I have ever taken to Las Vegas, I have always gone out around midnight and hung around the entrance to the Miracle Mile Shops. Across the street from the Bellagio Fountains is an area that sees a lot of foot traffic and plenty of interesting characters. The shops themselves exit right onto the strip but are elevated a bit, so you have to take an escalator down to the sidewalk. There are railings you can lean over and just stand by, and people watch. I would often come out here and just watch all of the different people coming in and out of the hotel and walking the street.

Depending on the time of night, you'd also get people dressed in Hello Kitty or Mickey Mouse costumes trying to get tourists to take photos with them for tips. On the more risqué side, you'd also see women dressed as showgirls, or "sexy cops" or basically any kind of provocative costume you can think of trying to entice the public, usually men, to stop and take a photo with them for a tip.

Whether it's watching the nervous guys around the girls, or the drunk people trying to wade through the crowds, or other people busking and trying to get a tip or two, just standing around and observing the varying degrees of excess has always been entertaining and something I love to do.

When I got back to the hotel, I told Ken that I was just going to go out for a walk, but it wasn't just that. In some ways, I'm very much an introvert. I do enjoy my time being alone. It's not that I don't like people, but there are times when I really just need to be by myself with my own thoughts. Having spent the last week with these three great friends, I really just wanted some time on my own, and although the strip would have a ton of people around it, for those few minutes, I could focus purely on watching the crowds and doing whatever I wanted.

After peering across the street for quite a while, I turned and started walking along the upper portion towards the down escalators and spotted two girls dressed in what could only be described as the skimpiest police uniforms. A quick request and tip later, I snapped a photo and then wandered over to the Bellagio to see the fountains. I watched the water show, wandered back across the street, and knew it was time for bed. By the time I got back to the hotel, I was ready to hit the sack as I knew we'd be starting our next leg the following morning.

For me, I wished we had been able to spend more time in Las Vegas. It's a city that is closely becoming a bit of a rival to New York for me but for entirely different reasons. New York is a city that I feel like I could just be absorbed into and love every moment of it, whereas Las Vegas draws me in for its ability to somehow allow me to forget who I am and escape into another world even if it is just for a few days. Whenever I visit, it feels like I am releasing the person I am back at home for a few days while I disappear into the escapism that this city seems to provide. Whenever I find myself in need of evading reality, Las Vegas is there. But for now, at least, I was looking forward to starting the journey back home the next day.

The Earth,
The Skies
& Cars Disguised

> September 11th, 2017
>
> The journey home begins with a couple of amazing pit stops along the way.

Las Vegas may have been halfway through our two-week trek, but it also served as a virtual turning point for us on this trip. The entire journey west had felt like we were encountering one thing after another that was new, exciting, or interesting. It always seemed that there was yet one more milestone we were trying to hit as we were traveling west.

But when our time in Vegas was over, the number of milestone locations to hit on the eastern journey back towards home was far fewer. We had pegged Amarillo Texas, Pensacola Florida, and New York City as our three significant stops on the way back, but there were only a handful of things we really wanted to see while we were heading east: The Grand Canyon, The Four Corners, The Cadillac Ranch, downtown Washington D.C., and New York City. Beyond that, whatever we happened to encounter along the way, plus the actual geocaches we would snag, would be all that we were looking for on that end of the journey.

Before the trip had even begun, I suspected that once we were done Las Vegas, the rest of the trip would probably be a bit of a blur, or at the very least, far less exciting. Traveling west, we were full of ambition to try and get there as fast as we could as almost all of the biggest things we wanted to see were on that portion of the trip. With so few items of interest to us on the return, I suspected we would spend more time just driving and pushing through than we would actually see much of anything. It turns out, that was the case, after all.

On Monday morning, we got up, packed our stuff, and hit the I-15 towards Arizona. We had already snagged this state for geocaches, but the plan was to head out and see the North Rim of The Grand Canyon that day. Ken had actually plotted a new route that gave us time to see the canyon and still get the states we needed from the area. The only catch was getting out of the canyon area would require us to take some secondary highways, which would slow us down a bit.

Even though we had already found our necessary caches for Arizona, we kept our eye on the map to see if any would pop up along our route. The drive along the state highway was about as desert as it can get. There wasn't much in the way of wildlife or even greens to be seen, yet it still had a beauty all of its own.

We opted to stop for a geocache not far from the Virgin River. Finding the container was easy, but it was the Desert Mountains that struck me as I turned around to go back to the car. Mountains of any kind can be quite beautiful, but often folks will think of the Rockies or the Alps, which are typically covered in or at least speckled in snow. Desert Mountains look pretty plain and vanilla in comparison to something like the Rockies, but they have their own kind of beauty.

Often when someone takes a photo of a mountain, you don't really get to see the perspective of the size of the rock compared to a person unless the picture includes a reference point. I stood at the shrub where the container had been hidden and snapped this photo of Mark heading back towards the car. There may not have been any snow on that hill, but it certainly stood out as being quite a fantastic sight. The drive continued through many similar mountains, and I made a note of it in my journal to make sure I didn't forget it.

Continuing past the Hurricane Valley Mountains, we hit a lot of rural roads as we snaked our way down towards the North Rim. Literally, in the middle of nowhere, we found a little village called Fredonia, which we could only spot one store which happened to be a dollar store. A few more minutes up the road, we heard a huge roar rip from the sky. We spotted an F-16 fighter doing what looked like a practice run of some kind up in the sky. Turkeys, cows, bison, and some deer were seen in various points along this desert trek.

We eventually hit the North Rim of the canyon, found a spot to park the car, and went for a walk. There were a handful of trails that we could follow that would give us some pretty spectacular views of the canyon. On one side, there was a little bit of railing and a small structure with a few outcrops you could stand out on and take in the view. The other end provided another great view of the canyon, but there were some side paths where people had gone up onto the rocks to get a better look and snap some photographs.

I don't want to say that I was the most adventurous one, but I will say that I was the one who hopped onto some of these lesser than safe ledges to see the view and snapped a few photographs. In fact, I remember Ken feeling quite uncomfortable about getting anywhere near the edge of some of those lookouts. I handed my camera to one of the boys and asked them to take a couple of photos for me showing the perspective of where I was in comparison to the canyon. Truth be told, I actually was trying to recreate one of my favorite photographs I had taken on a vacation overseas.

I don't remember who was behind me taking the photo, but I do remember that the view from standing there looking out into the abyss reminded me an awful lot of what it was like standing at the top of "The High Place of Sacrifice" in Petra, Jordan. The view here was just as spectacular and gave me pause to realize that the boys and I were indeed incredibly lucky to be able to have the chance to see this spot together.

What you don't see here is the photograph of the four of us at the edge of the lookout together, and that's because of what I chose to wear that day. I have been known to wear t-shirts with less than favorable or perhaps unique quotes on them. By unique, some people would see them as obscene or offensive. I had made a joke to my wife about the "Keep Calm" shirts that you see all over the place. I had said someone should make one that says "Keep Calm and …" but with something much more graphic on the end. Not long later, my wife presents me with this exact shirt as a gift. That day out at the canyon, I wore it during our excursion, and all of our group photos have that clearly visible on the front. It certainly makes the photos memorable, albeit a bit inappropriate.

By the time we left the Grand Canyon, our next hopeful stop was supposed to be the infamous "Four Corners" monument. This spot is where Arizona, Utah, Colorado, and New Mexico all meet in one specific geographic location. It's a well-known landmark where you can actually stand in a spot and be in all four states at the same time. We needed to push as hard as we could to get there as we didn't know if the actual monument could be reached during off-hours, and we knew it would likely be night time when we got there.

On our journey to the corners, we passed by Marble Canyon, where the Navajo Bridge is located. This bridge is a nice walking bridge that takes you from one side of the Colorado River to the other. Again, this was another great spot to visit, and we were only passing through, so we parked the car, wandered around, took some photographs, bought some swag from the locals, and then continued on our way.

Unfortunately, the highway we were on was a secondary highway that weaved in and out of the surrounding terrain. As lovely as it was to see the view and watch the sun go down from the road, it was taking a toll on our time to get to our destination for that night. There were entire stretches where we had the van well above the speed limit, hoping to gain some extra mileage, but then we'd come by a crazy turn and realize we needed to slow down. By the time we got to the actual four corners, we had come to find out it was closed and blocked off by fences and gates with no way to get in to see the real monument. Of all the spots we had wanted to see, this was the only one on our list that we didn't catch on our trip. It did, however, provide an unexpected opportunity to observe something we hadn't seen yet.

If you can, punch in this destination into Google Maps and bring up the Street View: 36° 59.599'N 109° 2.459'W. These coordinates take you to the actual entrance to the Four Corners Monument. In Street View, you can actually see the sign for the entry. When you look at that spot from Street View, you can clearly see that there's absolutely nothing around. It literally is in the middle of nowhere with no real buildings, no street lights, and nothing to be seen anywhere. Now, imagine what this place would have looked like at night.

When we arrived here, it was a little after 10:00 pm local time, and there was no way of getting inside. We paused for a moment and then took a look up at the sky. In the middle of the New Mexico desert, with no light pollution from anywhere, you could see every single star in the night time sky. All four of us got real silent for a moment as we realized how incredibly beautiful the heavens were, and how quiet it was all around us. With the van turned off, and us mesmerized, I took a few steps away, sat down on the gravel, and then laid flat out looking straight up.

I had seen the stars plenty of times back home while out for a drive at night. But never in all my life had I seen the sky like this. It made me realize that I really should invest in getting some glasses to perceive distances a bit better, but despite that, I just laid there for a few minutes taking in the moment. From this point onward, we had nowhere we had to be or get to, it was now merely just pushing onward towards our next major city, and we wouldn't be getting anywhere near that until the following day anyway so why not just soak up everything there was to see in the sky even if it was just for a moment. We all knew that we would have to get back on the road again, but much like the amazement of the trees in California, the stars took our breath away for a few moments before we had to point the car south to Albuquerque.

After not being able to snag the four corners, our spirits were a bit on the low side, but seeing the sites of the night time sky lifted them enough that hitting the road felt just fine to us. We actually turned around and headed directly south, taking another secondary highway, the 491, down towards the I-40, which would then take us into Albuquerque. It was going to be a little more than four hours of a drive to get there, and it felt even longer on that highway. There were spots on the roadway where there was no passing, or the speed limit was far lower than we wanted. Even though it was falling into the middle of the night with barely a soul on the road, we still felt like a turtle crawling in the dirt.

When the I-40 finally came, we took the opportunity to get our first official New Mexico geocache and get a glimpse of something extra along the way. Route 66 actually runs along the same stretch of highway that we were traveling, so when we took exit 20 to try and find some local caches, we all spotted the unique sign on the road. The famous route 66 markers had been painted directly onto the street itself, and although in some spots it was hard to see, it was still cool to see a part of history. Unfortunately, we struck out with the first two caches we tried to find, including one hidden near some rail tracks with railway related artifacts spread out across the front lawn. We opted to snag the far simpler park and grab (park the car, and quickly find the container) up the street before moving along. We kept on the same route 66 for a while until we eventually came upon a closed gas station in the middle of the night that had a cache hidden just off to the side.

By the time we hit Albuquerque, both Ken & Paul were asleep in the back, and the clock had struck right around 3:00 am or so. I had hoped we would have gone through here in the daytime as I had been to this place several times for work. I thought it would have been a cool photo of the 4 Guys standing outside of Walter White's house (from Breaking Bad). But alas, with the boys asleep, I talked to Mark while he was driving and told him a few stories about having been in the area before.

It's actually quite a charming city with the view from the Sandia Peak Tramway up the hill. The company I work for brought a bunch of us up there for dinner during one work event, and I really enjoyed the food and the view. Definitely a place to go visit if you are in the area, but avoid it at all costs if you're afraid of heights.

As we passed by the intersection for I-25, I told Mark that our office was "just up the street over there" as I pointed, and then before we knew it, we had left the city limits. Our next destination was just outside of Amarillo, Texas.

Known as the Cadillac Graveyard, this field is right smack in the middle of prime farmland, and believe me, you could smell it from any direction. We parked the car just off the highway and made our way down to the graveyard, where we did indeed see a collection of old Cadillac vehicles that had been placed vertically and then spray painted. Many others had brought their own paint and done their own take on the cars. We put a few "4 Guys" stickers on several of the cars and snapped as many photos as we could. Ultimately, this would end up being the last major "destination" until we hit DC.

Unlike previous legs, we didn't have an exact spot or location in mind that we wanted to get to before calling it a night. We just knew that we wanted to continue to drive until we were ready to stop. Interestingly enough, we made a minor unexpected pit stop in

Oklahoma City that would have us working on the car and checking out a nearby shop. Paul had mentioned wanting to see F & A Creations, which was right in the area, so we popped in, and he took a few photos. But the most unusual thing about this pit stop was taking the van for an oil change.

At this point, we had clocked more than 10,000kms onto the odometer of that poor van. Ken had made a couple of comments before the trip about how we would be pushing the van past its regular oil change time. Now for me, it was a rental, and I didn't see the need to do the change as I figured that was in the hands of the rental company.

But the reality is we were putting the van through a hell of a lot of miles, so I suppose it would be a kind courtesy to get the oil changed while on our journey. So we stopped at a Jiffy Lube right on Meridian Ave and then went for a walk to snag the two geocaches that were within walking distance. By the time we finished finding those caches, the oil change was done, and we were on our way.

By this point in the day, we were getting a bit fatigued and decided that Little Rock would be our official stop for the night.

We rolled into a rest stop on the other side of the Arkansas border and snapped a photo of Ken in his famous horse mask. Many of the state signs we had taken pictures of included Ken in his mask, but his ultimate goal was always trying to be able to relieve himself in every state. I don't know if he got all 48, but I know he got pretty close.

When we finally came into the hotel that night, we really wanted to get some food. Trying to find a decent place to eat anywhere in the area was challenging, to say the least. Eventually, we hit up a Sonic, which ended up being a bit of a pain in the ass with low-quality food and not excellent service as I recall. At the time, though, it really didn't matter because we just needed some kind of grub to hold us over. Once we had some food, we hit the hotel, crashed, and would make our way to Washington DC the next day.

Move Along Nothing to See Here

September 13th, 2017

An entire portion of the trip that most of us have no memory of.

In deciding to write about this trip, I knew that this particular leg would likely be the one that would be the hardest to write about. Not because of any tragedy or emotional distress that was encountered, but only because from this point until D.C., we didn't have anything notable to see or do other than the finding of the actual geocaches we needed for each state. This was a leg of the journey that was born purely out of necessity. We had to take the route we took and travel through where we did because we needed geocaches for these states and nothing else. So in recollection of what was most memorable about this leg, there are entire portions of it that I don't recall either because I was sleeping through it or nothing notable was seen or experienced during that time.

Mark, Ken, and Paul all made mention of minor things we experienced, but they too found this leg harder to recall many of the details than any other portion of the trip. This further reinforced the idea that although this trip was supposed to be about geocaching, the actual finding of containers was far less exciting than all of the other things we saw and experienced. But for this leg, we still had to get going and make our way closer to D.C. and New York City.

That morning, we got up and knew that our next official destination was going to be Wilmington, Delaware. Not because we deemed it as an exciting place to get to (no offense to those who live there), but because I had booked two rooms at a Hilton Hotel downtown on points for us, and it was close enough to New York we knew we'd be able to get there relatively easy while snagging a bunch of state caches on the way. But before getting there, we had a bit of a trek to go through.

This leg of the trip consisted of traveling through the infamous "bible belt" of the US. We had already entered this portion of the country, but within the next two days, we'd pass through most of it and spot some interesting sights along the way.

One spot was the Louisiana Cotton Museum, located in Lake Providence Louisiana. I had never seen a cotton field before, and here we were right in the middle of cotton country. We popped into this local museum and discovered that someone had hidden a geocache on the property, with permission of course, in the "outhouse" near the parking area. We all got a good laugh out of the placement of the cache, but then looked around the area and museum a bit more to take in what the place had to offer. We spoke to the friendly caretaker who asked us if we were taking his "pehcauns". He then told us about almost having been to Canada once to retrieve a stolen tractor from Rochester but found it far too cold up there. Not long after that, we drove through a place called Transylvania, which much to our disappointment did not have any vampires.

By this time, we were getting hungry and were coming through a place called Tallulah. We were trying to find a place to get some southern BBQ, but we had somehow stumbled upon a pretty rundown neighborhood. In fact, both Paul and I were getting a little uncomfortable with the surroundings. We took a corner, and Ken spotted a restaurant called "Sugas". Both Mark and Ken seemed keen on going in to get some food, but neither Paul nor I were getting out of the car. The building looked like an ancient trailer from a rundown trailer park with the name "Sugas" spray-painted across the side. That was enough for both of us to veto any chance of going inside to get some food. Long after the trip was over, I looked the place up on Google, and sure enough, it is listed as a delicious restaurant with great prices and fantastic food. The Street View on Google Maps also showed that the sign was not actually spray painted. Thinking about it now, I suspect I thought it was spray-painted based on the way it looked and the surrounding neighborhood. I'm sure it would have been fine, but for both Paul & I, we just didn't like the area we were in and wanted to go somewhere we felt a bit more secure. We ultimately settled on the buffet up the road at the Love's Travel Stop, which ended up having some fantastic food and where I was able to acquire some hot sauces for my father-in-law.

Once we hit the I-20, it was eastbound towards Mississippi and then onwards to Alabama and eventually into Florida. Traveling through those southern states and then through Florida and upwards towards Georgia and the Carolinas is all a bit of a fog for the four of us with only spots here and there that  seem to stand out. Spotting prisoners in black and white jumpsuits, billboards with the Ten Commandments, and plenty of dead animals on the side of the road were about the only things I made a note of in my journal.

Beyond that, the only parts of that section of the trip that stood out were things that Ken & Paul have since mentioned. In digging through my photos, I came across one that we had taken of this tiny little frog that we found at a lamp post cache in Pensacola Florida. We had seen a bit of wildlife here and there, but this was our closest encounter to date.

Paul tells the story of driving along the highway and having to follow the big transport trucks due to the road hazards. It turns out there were so many dead deer along the side of the road that it was just more comfortable to sit behind the rigs so they could act as battering rams against anything that might jump out. As Paul recalls, "…and then a firebird passed me and hit a deer just a bit after. The deer was on the road dead, and the car was pulled over on the left side of the road." Ken also tells the story of driving through Atlanta and having eight lanes of traffic all to himself while blowing through there in the middle of the night and spotting the massive Kia plant. The only thing I can remember about Atlanta is waking up, seeing the lights of the city, and then putting my head back down and going back to sleep.

It really wasn't until we hit Tennessee and West Virginia where things start to focus in a bit more. There was a geocache we snagged just off I-40 on the Tennessee/North Carolina border that I had forgotten about until Paul and Ken reminded me. The geocache was hidden just off the road and into the woods a bit, but it was what we found near the cache that surprised us. There was a considerable portion of a deer carcass on the ground right beside the cache. The head was surprisingly well intact with the eyes and antlers clearly visible, but only the ribcage really remained beyond that. A bonus to finding this cache in this particular spot was that we had walked on a portion of the Appalachian Trail to get to it. This granted us permission to now say we had "hiked" on that famous trail.

We continued north towards Kentucky, where we snagged a few more caches and then headed east towards West Virginia. Because of the particular route we had opted to take, it ended up being an extended drive through Norton, Castlewood, and Bluefield. West Virginia isn't known for its high population of people, but one thing we did see plenty of was green.

Scattered along the roadways were endless runs of vines,

trees, grass, and greenery that seemed to just go from infinity to beyond (no Buzz Lightyear to be seen). Entire portions of the hills and trees were utterly engrossed in nothing more than long vines of solid green leaves. We never did stop to admire it, but it certainly made an impression as we got to see the ins and outs of most of southern West Virginia.

After taking what felt like forever to get through, we finally hit Maryland and worked onwards to DC. The intention all along had been to try and spend a little bit of time in DC to snag a bunch of the virtual caches along with catching any of the major sites while we had the chance. Unfortunately, the timing for us in DC didn't work out to our advantage, and we didn't get to spend as much time as we had wanted.

When we rolled into the nation's capital, night had set in, and we knew we still had to make it as far as Delaware that evening. We looped around downtown a bit and did manage to park the car long enough to both grab a regular geocache hidden near a high-end hotel, as well as snag two virtual caches in the area. A few photo snaps later, we got back in the car and knew we had two more caches and one more stop to make before calling it a night. It was a bit disappointing having to leave DC that quickly, but we had at least made it there and had been able to see even just a smidge of it. Before we knew it, we had snagged our two caches for Maryland and were pulling into the Doubletree Hotel in Wilmington, Delaware.

I had used my frequent stay points to book two rooms for us

at this hotel as I had stayed there before. The boys had seen a video I had posted on YouTube when on assignment for work in Wilmington earlier that year. A severe snowstorm came through the city while I was there to deliver a class. On day two of training, the class was canceled because of the "storm". As a Canadian from Moncton, I had experienced my share of heavy snow winters where storms would drop a couple of feet of snow on the ground, and people would barely blink at it. So when I was in Wilmington and their "storm" hit, I was thinking a storm like back home, but their version consisted of two inches of snow on the ground and everything in town being closed for the day.

With no snow this time, the hotel was a welcome roof over our heads for the night and was close enough to Philadelphia, New Jersey, and New York that it wouldn't take much time to drive where we were heading the next day. After getting checked in, we all went to go crash but had our sleep diverted temporarily when the hotel fire alarm went off around midnight, forcing everyone out of the hotel while the fire department conducted a search and review of the building. Much to everyone's annoyance, the alarms had gone off because someone had been smoking in their room. Once we got back inside, we were out cold for the night. The next day would see a few quick stops to get a few caches then push our way to New York City.

From Traveler to Local in One Ride

> September 15th, 2017
>
> Our last major stop before heading home included some great memories.

By 10:09 in the morning, we had left the hotel and were doing our best to do a quick park and grab for two caches in downtown Wilmington. One of the caches we found was one I had not been able to find when I had been there earlier in the year and turned out to be far easier to find than I had initially thought. We crossed Delaware off our list and headed north up the I-95 and on our way into New Jersey. At first, it was more about just getting two caches and parking the car, but then we had a couple of detours. The first one was minor in that we snagged one cache in a place called New Brunswick.

Having come from a province named New Brunswick, it only seemed appropriate that we take a photo in front of the sign welcoming people to their city. It only took a minute or two to make the detour, and we all got a good kick out of it.

The second detour was one I wasn't all that keen on. The truth is, I really wanted to get into New York City. Of all places I have been to in the world, New York is at the top of my all-time favorites list. It's a place I never tire of and was anxious to get us there. But the boys wanted to make a pit stop and try and pick up some alcohol, and as someone who doesn't drink, it wasn't something I was overly interested in. On our way to Costco, we got yelled at by some crazy lady who cut in front of us at the toll plaza but somehow thought we were in the wrong. Items were acquired at Costco shortly thereafter and then we headed into the Big Apple. In retrospect, had we arrived in NYC earlier, I would not have had one of my favorite experiences of that trip, so I suppose it was the universe intervening somehow. That would come a few hours later, but for now, the boys needed their booze, and we blew through Costco quickly enough.

Once that was out of the way, we drove right up to Secaucus New Jersey, parked the car at the train station, and bought tickets into the city. It was a hell of a lot easier to take the train into Manhattan than to drive there and try to find parking. Plus, we already knew that when we were done, we would be taking the I-95 out of there anyway, so why not just avoid city traffic entirely.

The train from Jersey takes you right to Penn Station in midtown Manhattan. Given that we had a limited amount of time, it was best to maximize our exploration of the city. As I recall, Paul had never been to NYC as an adult and had only visited many years ago when he was in school, so I wanted to try and make sure he got to see whatever it was he wanted. So, for him, we went straight to Central Park and started at Columbus Circle and made our way through the park and eventually came out at Strawberry Fields & The Dakota right along Central Park West & 72nd Street. With a limited amount of time, we couldn't see the whole park, but we did manage to cover a good portion of the bottom third of the area.

The next stop was Times Square and Grand Central Station. We popped into GCT just long enough to be able to snap some photos and say that we were there. But for Times Square, it was photo op time.

Getting the shot of the four of us at the Las Vegas sign or even the tunnel in Washington State marked our territory on that end of the country. This photo marked our arrival to the other end of the country and would serve as the last significant photograph of all four of us before we got back home. We had some food at the Hard Rock Café in Times Square and then made our way to our next destination: Ghostbusters Fire Hall.

We hit the subway and began our journey downtown. We had asked Paul several times about where he wanted to go in NYC, and every time he always mentioned that he wanted to see the Ghostbusters Fire Hall and see Central Park. With the park now behind us, and timing ticking away on our visit to the Big Apple, it was time to head down to 14 N Moore St in Tribeca.

As an avid lover of NYC, every time I visit, I always picked one distinctive location that I want to go see or do that I had never done before. One time I went up to view the diner from Seinfeld. Another time it was a park in Queens used as the backdrop for the final battle in Men in Black. The last memorable location I went to see was the exterior building used for the "apartment" in Friends, which is located at the corner of Bedford and Grove.

The Ghostbusters Fire Hall was one of those locations I had picked to visit during one of my work assignments in NYC and had been back to it a few times. A quick Google search refreshed my memory on where it was and off to the subway we were.

We went into the subway station just near Times Square, went downstairs and waited for the train like anyone else. But this particular subway ride would result in one of my fondest memories of NYC of all time and set the song for this trip.

Wait, the song? What song?

For all of my major road trips over the years, there has always been a song or group of songs that I have associated with that trip. When I went to Toronto to see Faith No More play for the first time in 1995, "December" by Collective Soul and "Long View" from Green Day kept coming on the radio, so now I always associate those songs with that trip. Collective Soul's "Maybe" was a song I heard again and again while driving to Los Angeles in 1997. "Canary in a Coal Mine" was the song that my friend Cheez played on the car stereo repeatedly while we drove from Moncton to Croton-Harmon New York, back in 1996. So when we set out on our 48 state adventure, I wondered what song it might be. Although I am an avid music lover and have tastes that span from Burt Bacharach to Carcass, The Beatles are not a band I have ever enjoyed or spent any amount of time listening to. So, it came as a big surprise for one of their songs to end up being associated with a road trip of mine.

When we got on the subway, there wasn't any room for me to sit, so I stood and held onto one of the metal poles everyone uses to stay steady. As I waited for the doors to close, I noticed a man across from me with a guitar on his lap. A woman struck up a conversation with him and asked him to play a song. The doors closed, and as he started playing, she immediately said: "Oh, I love that song."

At first, I had no idea what the song was, but once he opened his mouth and started singing, I found myself remembering the song and began to chime in with him. Initially, I didn't remember all of the words, but for some reason, I recalled the lyrics from watching an episode of ER where Susan Lewis was singing "Blackbird" as her sister Chloe was giving birth. I have no idea why I remembered that particular scene, but there it was.

As I was singing with him, the woman who was talking to him before began singing along with her friend. None of us knew each other, but we all just broke out singing together as if we had known each other for years. For the couple of minutes that he played, I forgot where I was, who I was with, and all about the fact that we had just driven from Moncton to San Francisco and back to New York over the last 13 days. As I looked around the train car, there were the faces of strangers watching all of us with big smiles truly enjoying the impromptu singalong that had sprung out of a group of strangers meeting on a train. At some point during the song, the guy playing guitar looked at us and made a comment about us sounding like professionals because the harmonies sounded so nice. We all smiled at each other and continued to sing as the subway car bumped along the tracks heading down towards Ghostbusters HQ.

By that time, we had driven about 15,000kms around the US and were winding the trip down as we would be starting our final leg towards home that night. Our visit to NYC was the last of our major stops before we made the 14hr haul back to Moncton. I stood there, hanging on like any other passenger, looked around, and I couldn't stop smiling. Then just as quickly as it had started, the song was over, and the subway car erupted with applause. When the doors opened, and I knew we had to get off, I gave the guitar player a bunch of my American change and apologized to him for the lack of bills. He told me not to worry about it and thanked me for my generosity. I walked off the subway and onto the platform, and we headed upstairs to find the firehouse. For me, the song Blackbird would stick in my head for the rest of the trip home, and become the song that defined my "4 Guys in A Car" trip.

In those few minutes of standing on the train, singing to a group of strangers, I realized that I had just lost myself in a moment of pure immersion. I'd been in the van with Mark, Ken, and Paul for almost two full weeks, seeing all of these different places across the entire United States of America. But at that moment, on that train, on that car, with that group of people, I wasn't a Canadian traveler visiting NYC. I was a local resident jumping in on what countless others see and experience almost every day they ride the train in a city like that. I wasn't thinking about getting home, the long drive ahead, the countless photos I had taken, the places I had seen, or the memories I had made. I was just a guy on a train taking part in something bigger than any one of us alone.

I don't know if words can truly express why this single experience stuck with me. What I can say is that it was one of the few moments I have had while traveling where I can honestly say that I genuinely felt like I had somehow just magically become a part of the city, even if it was only between train stops.

A few days after I finally returned home, I went on iTunes and looked for Blackbird. I chose the Sarah McLaughlin version as it just seemed closer to what I had felt on the train. As soon as the song was downloaded, I played it, and my mind immediately went back to that subway car. There was no doubt now that this song would be the one I'd always associate with my "4 Guys In A Car" trip.

The visit to the fire hall itself was pretty run of the mill for me but still a highlight given that Paul had really wanted to see this place. Although there was construction obstructing part of the front of the building, it was still a nice little stop along the way. Plus, had we not decided to come to the hall, I may never have had that memorable experience on the subway.

Our last stop in NYC before catching the train back to Jersey was a brand new virtual geocache that had just been published less than a month prior. It was located at the 9/11 memorial park in downtown NYC near the financial district. Although it was the virtual cache that brought us there, this is always a nice place to visit and remember what happened on that fateful day. While the park is quite something to see now, I had been in NYC less than a year after the attacks and had visited the remains of the twin towers. It didn't matter where you walked around the rubble; you could just feel what had happened there. I remember coming home and telling my then-girlfriend that it "just felt like death everywhere." Thankfully, this fantastic memorial park they have created is an authentic tribute to those lost and made for a charming final stop on our NYC tour.

Reflecting on it now, I think our little mini-tour of NYC was just what the four of us needed to push us towards the finish line. A lot of time and distance had been covered over the last few days, but it had yielded very little in the way of exciting sights or notable memories. We were all getting tired and really knew that we just had to push forward, and we would be home in no time flat. With fatigue on our minds, and wanting to get closer to home, we really needed something to give us that jolt of energy to keep moving. New York City provided that in spades.

After snapping a few photos of the new Freedom Tower as seen from the park, we headed back to the subway and onward to the train station. Before I knew it, we were back at the van and ready to start the final leg of this two-week trip.

The Longest Journey

September 15th, 2017

With only a handful of states left, it was time to make our way back to where we started.

Our visit to NYC, as well as the final trip back home, was all formerly part of the same leg, but I always felt like the moment we left the Big Apple signaled the official last leg of our journey. It must have been somewhere around 9:00 pm or so when we got back in the car and pointed it north. We only had three more states to go (Connecticut, Rhode Island, and Massachusetts) before we could officially say that we had done all 48 states. There were only about 13 or 14 hours left of driving, which felt like a small amount compared to what we had done before, but this would be the last of the long hauls of driving, then we'd be back to our hometown.

We set out on I-95, which we'd be able to follow all the way back to Canada. If we had been going directly home, it would likely have been faster to hop on the I-91 and I-84, but we had to circle around the states to make our way to Providence Rhode Island, and then head up towards Boston. After what felt like the blink of an eye, we had already snagged a couple caches in Connecticut and kept on rolling. It was actually Rhode Island that gave us a batch of DNFs that frustrated us more than anything.

After having cached across the country and back, we had been pretty lucky in that we hadn't had to deal with very many "Did Not Finds" or DNFs as geocachers refer to them. But it was as if the geocaching gods had looked down on us and decided that it was time for a bit of DNF torture. It seemed the first handful of caches we tried to find in this state were nowhere to be found. In the middle of rural Rhode Island, each time we would stop to get yet one more cache, we were coming up short. I suspect the anxiousness of wanting to get home probably contributed to our lack of success in that state. When we finally did get our two caches, we were all more than happy to finally have them done and were ready to cross that last state off the list.

As we cruised up the 95 heading towards Boston, we decided that the best thing to do was put on some good old fashion comedy. Ken dug out a copy of Eddie Murphy's "Delirious" set from the 1980's. We'd all heard the set countless times before, but at this time of night and getting closer to home, we needed something classic to keep us entertained. Having watched the VHS of that stand-up countless times as a teenager, I remembered most of it as it came out of the speakers, but I had never heard the other guys laugh that hard. Between the jokes about Mr. T & Aunt Bunny, I started to wonder if we'd be pulling into a hospital to have Ken treated for a coronary from laughing so hard.

Not long after passing into Massachusetts, we rolled into an old abandoned rest stop where we snagged our first of two caches for the state and officially completed our mission. Our website, www.4guysinacar.com, had been updating the entire trip showing our progress for caches found along with which states we had acquired based on the logged caches. When we finally made it to the I-495 and snagged that cache, the website updated and displayed the message "All 48 states and DC acquired". This was the entire point of the trip, and we could now focus entirely on making our way back to Moncton. Once we got around to the northern side of the 495, we snagged one more cache, and that was the end to the geocaching portion of the trip. I dug out my list of states I had been crossing off during the journey and drew a line through Massachusetts to mark it off and got a massive grin on my face. This was it. We had done it. Now we just had to get home.

Coming out of New Hampshire and heading into Maine, Mark and I noticed the dense fog. Aside from a bit of rain near the tail end of our first Maine crossing, nighttime weather had been pretty clear for the entire trip. Even with the heavy smell of smoke in the Pacific Northwest, traveling the highways at night had been, for the most part, clear. As we crossed the border into Maine, Ken & Paul were half asleep in the back while Mark did the driving, and I helped him stay alert. The fog was thick and soupy in spots, and I assumed that as we got further north, it would start to lift. But even by the time we had passed Bangor and hit the airline road, the fog seemed to follow us. At this time of night, there was virtually no traffic which typically would have made the trek along that road go a bit faster, but with it being such a rural area in heavy fog, you always had to be a bit extra cautious wondering if some kind of wildlife was going to jump out in front of you.

When traveling north, the highway ends at an intersection where an Irving Big Stop gas station sits waiting for those who need a fill-up before crossing the border. That gas station was always a stopping point for me whether I was going into or out of the US. In fact, we had stopped there on our way out and were now working our way back. All I had to do was find the truck on a pole, and I'd know we were close.

Having become extra familiar with the airline road during my one year stay in the US, I had made a note of one unusual landmark on that highway. About 15 minutes into your journey south on the #9, you'd drive by what looked like a regular telephone pole. But as you passed it, you'd notice that it was an actual work truck sitting atop of the pole. The "truck on a pole" became a marker to look for when traveling north to let you know you were about to hit the big stop.

By this time, the sun was trying to come up, and the fog had finally started to lift. Ken & Paul had woken up, and we were all thinking about breakfast and knew we were now less than four hours from home. We parked the car at the gas station, went inside to the restaurant, and ordered some food. Not only did the gas fill the car up, the food fueled us for the next part of our journey: we knew there would be no other stops until we got home. We got to the border and had no issues coming back into Canada. With the signs now all reading kilometers and not miles, all four of us could feel the sigh of relief as we got closer to home.

We'd had a great trip and seen a ton of amazing sights along the way. But the mere crossing of the US-Canada border into St. Stephen somehow felt like a weight had been lifted off of our shoulders. Although we never experienced any significant obstacles or roadblocks along our two-week trek, and I really don't think any of us had any major worries, the realities of traveling that much distance meant that there were plenty of things that could have gone wrong. Getting back into Canada meant that there really were no more obstacles to overcome, and all we had to do was just get the van a couple hundred more kilometers to make it home.

Those last three hours blew by in no time flat, and before we knew it, we had chosen to take River Rd through Salisbury to take the back way home instead of the regular Trans-Canada highway. One of the reasons why I remember wanting to take that back road was to be able to stop at the "Welcome to Riverview" sign. All four of us live in Riverview, and this was really a way for us to put one

last photo on the reel and bring the entire trip to a complete close. As it turned out, we had one more surprise waiting for us on the other end of town.

Ken had rented the van, and so he was the one who needed to return it, which meant the rest of us would be dropped off, and he'd bring the van home. He had decided it was easier to bring me and

Mark home first as we were on the far end of the town of Riverview and literally only a minute or so apart. So, we drove all the way to the east end of town, and as we got closer to Mark's gas station, we started to notice that there was a sign in the parking lot waiting for us.

Much to our surprise, our wives made arrangements to gather

some of our friends and family to welcome all of us back to town with a big sign and giant group of people all standing around waiting for us. I was astonished but incredibly happy to see familiar faces and especially my own family. We gave a round of hugs, shook some hands, snapped some photos, and before I knew it, I was heading home with my wife and kids. The end had really come.

After spending two weeks on the road with three great guys, it was all over. I made a point of snapping a photo of the odometer inside the van to get a final kilometer count. The van had so much mileage on the trip counter that we had rolled it once. The final tally on distance to go from start to finish was 16,751 kilometers. I was looking forward to hearing the story from Ken about what would happen when he'd return the van to the rental company. It turns out that since they were closed when the van  was due, he never got to see their reaction. We did learn later that the van got parked in the back of the rental agency and then seemed to disappear after a few days. We suspect that it was sold to a dealer as the mileage on the car was so high compared to what average rentals would have had.

We all enjoyed a pleasant Sunday off, and on Monday morning, I went back to work like nothing new or exciting had just happened. It seemed a bit surreal that after such a monumental trip to just go back to my regular day to day life. Despite the normalcy of it all, nothing was ever going to be the same after having experienced a trip like that.

The Aftermath

> What were the biggest takeaways from taking a trip like this?

The Aftermath

It's been two years since taking that trip, but still, somehow, it feels like it was only a couple of weeks ago. Between writing this book and conversations that seem to pop up from time to time, much of the details of the trip are still fresh in my mind. I suspect that's why it still feels so recent to me. With the trip bringing us closer as friends, it's no surprise that it comes up in conversation more often than we'd expect. I've found myself smiling while out with any of the guys, and the topic of our road trip bubbles to the surface in the most random of conversations.

With having so many vivid memories of being in all these different places and the sheer intensity and absurdity of the whole thing, in many ways, it feels very surreal and almost unbelievable that we undertook such an amazing adventure together. Enough time has passed that in some ways, it feels a lot more like a dream than reality. As the days pass, it becomes harder to recall the finite details about where we were and what we saw and what we did. But then someone will make a comment in passing, and all of a sudden, a flood of memories of sitting in that van will hit, and a big smile will come across my face. I chose to write all of this down so that regardless of what the future brings, there would be some sort of written account of our adventure across the United States. For all we know, we might all end up old and senile and have no recollection of ever having taken this trip. Hopefully, this story will help remind us of at least some parts of that long journey.

It also wasn't lost on me how a considerable portion of this trip reminded me of the first time I had traveled across the United

States. I didn't realize it when we made plans, but somewhere in the middle of that trip, I remembered that it was actually 20 years ago that summer that I took a road trip from Moncton to Los Angeles, to Vancouver, and then back to Moncton over three weeks. I had set out on my own, driving solo, to cover that entire distance with my own car and $2,000 to my name. In my early 20s, I knew that I may not ever get the chance to make a trip like that again in my lifetime, so I went for it. I found it incredibly satisfying to know that 20 years later, I was still finding ways to make trips like this possible. Plus, I can tell you that traveling by car with three other people was a hell of a lot more fun than doing it solo.

Having experienced this kind of trip now twice in my lifetime, I can tell you that aside from some of the same scenery and highways that we may have covered, there is one overwhelmingly common lesson I have learned from experiences such as this; It's that regardless of what you have going on in your life, and whatever means you have available to you, nothing is more powerful than a person's own drive to accomplish a goal. When you set your sights on something you want to do, don't lose sight of it, don't lose focus on it, then there's nothing that can get in your way.

I was 23, working as a delivery driver for Greco Pizza and living with my mom in 1997. Yet somehow, I found a way to save enough money to drive a car across two countries and back by myself. At the age of 43, with a family and all the responsibilities of life, I still found a way to execute an insane two-week trek across all 48 states, making it back in one piece and still being able to call those I shared the trip with my friends. All of that happened because I set a goal for myself, and I never lost sight of it. Since that first Canada Day evening down at the cottage, we planned a fantastic trip and never let it go, and because we focused on accomplishing what we all really wanted, we found a way to make it happen. And now it's part of my life's story. Some days it doesn't feel real, but other days, I just smile and wonder what may come next.

I think it's also fair to say that another major takeaway from this trip was the bond it created between the four of us. Ken and I were good friends before this trip and remain so today. But having spent so much time in the van with both Paul & Mark, I got to know them so much more so than I ever did before. I learned a lot more about Paul's interest in cars and more of his own personal history. I loved hearing Mark's stories about working at the funeral home and some of the unique things he had experienced there. Even getting to see the fearful side of Ken as we rounded that mountain in California provided a bit more depth to who he is. A trip like this was either going to strengthen or kill friendships and for us, I think it brought all of us closer together.

Since returning, there have been a few talks about taking another road trip, but nothing definitive has been planned yet. One idea that has gained a bit of traction is flying out to Vegas and use it as a starting point for a few treks from there to some of the national parks and other notable areas in the western states. We'd cap the trip off with a finale of spending a few days in LA. Paul has said he'd love to do the whole thing again and maybe even a tour across

Canada and back.

But as of this writing, it looks like our next trek is most likely to happen in August of 2020, with the four of us taking on Western Canada with a minor return trip to Seattle. Groundspeak is putting on a 20th-anniversary celebration of geocaching on August 15th, 2020, in Seattle. The following Saturday, GeoWoodstock, the largest annual geocaching event, will be held in Abbotsford, B.C. We plan to fly to Vancouver, rent a car, and drive to Seattle to attend the anniversary event. From there, we'll turn back towards Canada and drive up towards Alaska, the Yukon, and Northwest Territories and return to B.C. via Alberta and the Rocky Mountains to attend GeoWoodstock. We'd be able to cross off our last US state for which we can drive to, along with two of the three northern territories in Canada. For me, crossing Alaska off my list would allow me to finally complete my entire US state map, having already found geocaches in Hawaii several years ago.

I do, however, have one other massive road trip idea I'd like to execute but may take a few years before I can find a way to make it happen. Trying to tackle as many countries in Eastern Europe as possible within two weeks is something that I would love to be able to do. It's an entirely different kind of trip with different challenges, but I think it would make an incredible sequel to our journey across the 48 states. I'll have to see if it's in the cards to try and make that happen down the road.

For now, I am content to have experienced such an incredible journey with three great friends and to have been able to share my story with those who have chosen to read it. I'm looking forward to whatever new adventure comes along my way next.

APPENDIX I – Geocache List

For those who may be interested in the geocaches we found while on our trek, here is a map of the caches across the country we found, along with a list of the names and GC codes for each found cache.

GC10174 - Where There's Smoke 3

GC1169 - Mission 9: Tunnel of Light

GC12EC - Six feet OVER?!

GC13GN9 - Push the Michigan Limits - South

GC13J2T - Bowling For Caches!!!

GC178XT - Mirrored

GC19M0Z - Maryland House--TB Hotel (Version 4.0)

GC1BXF2 - Manny Zita

GC1CN8D - King Cotton

APPENDIX I – Geocache List

GC1CN8Z - Transylvania

GC1DC24 - Florida Style

GC1E0KY - FDIC #7

GC1H2MM - At rest

GC1HTTV - MOrest

GC1J9G2 - Piggies

GC1JW6D - WEST GARDINER SERVICE PLAZA

GC1MM5J - I'm Down

GC1QEDJ - Lunch with Lewis and Clark

GC1R453 - State Line

GC1V949 - NO RADARS only GPS

GC1VN84 - Stop & Go

GC1WV5Q - 95 NORTH

GC1XEAM - Coteau des Prairies

GC1Z1XG - **Stop n Go**

GC1ZBAZ - Can You Hear Me Now

GC2018 - Tristate Marker

GC220Q0 - Back in a minute LPC

GC22MBM - Leave Nothing To Chance

GC23D1D - GRF#59

GC247DM - The Simpsons: Edna Krabappel- ABC's of caching

GC2E7RT - Roadside Bus Stop Series #2

GC2EF5 - Edison's Edification

GC2J1WC - Edge of Wally

GC2PK9D - Taz's Towaoc

GC2YND9 - Faith of Our Fathers

GC2YW3Q - Under the Boardwalk

GC2Z3E2 - Heritage of Faith

GC3170E - WarNinjas Pier 39 Cache! ðŸŽ

GC3499B - 3 States, 1 Cache

GC36AJQ - Dinosaur Train Geocache: Spinosaurus

GC3ABBX - There used to be a liquor store here I-93 North

GC3CA4G - Minnesota State Fruit: Honeycrisp Apple

GC3CH3W - Warthog Down River Crossing

GC3CJP7 - 26-Flower Power Trail

GC3DWRZ - its for you \road side assistance\

GC3HJGC - Standing Guard...

GC3QXRD - Old Lot

GC41YKN - Road Trip!!!!

GC433MY - Lakeview Welcome at the Welcome Center

GC44XWT - Wilmer Park

GC46JG8 - Fife

APPENDIX I – Geocache List

GC46JKV - The Back way to West Fargo

GC484C1 - Sleep Well

GC4AP4N - Cadillac Ranch Micro

GC4CE1 - MM MM Good

GC4E0RC - 95 North :)

GC4E94 - IN THE BELLY OF THE BEAST

GC4E95 - LAKE-VEGAS

GC4K4HK - Dekalb Oasis TB/Swag Hotel

GC4K7Y3 - Cadillac Ranch Cars

GC4PK2G - St.Benedicts Cemetery

GC4RNVV - The Guardian...

GC4RVN5 - It's All Fun & Games Until the COPS Show Up...

GC4Z523 - Maryland House VI--Have a Picnic (Version 2.0)

GC4ZJ9R - It's a \W\ thang

GC52PBR - Coffey Rest Area - Southbound

GC56YAD - There used to be a liquor store here I-93 South

GC58P0Z - Feel the Force 14

GC5BCZM - Your First Car

GC5C11M - West Bound And Down

GC5EX2W - Seth Smith House circa 1768

GC5HY6G - Gotta love the traffic

GC5QHGA - A Spark of Life Has Re-appeared in Bluefield, WV

GC5T5PA - The Mighty Rigs of Yesteryear

GC5YRC4 - Is this Seriously a CERES Cache???

GC5ZRAB - Cowboy's Gateway to Colorado

GC61ZBV - Visit South Dakota!

GC631DB - Minimal Expectations

GC63PQF - The Kindness of Chickens

GC66A0H - I-85 P&G

GC685C - Pipe Spring National Monument

GC6C7NR - KEEP It Alive!!

GC6CNN7 - Ahhhh. . .

GC6ETXT - Old Pony Express Bridge!

GC6F41Q - ALOHA FROM HAWAII - NV, LAS VEGAS

GC6GD8X - Marketplace

GC6J8AD - Clifton One and One

GC6K7D4 - Kouchibouguac National Park Geocaching

GC6KX4V - Freddie's Cache

GC6RC44 - Rhode Island, By Way Of Wyoming

GC6XNZZ - Battleship (RI) - B4

GC6ZDMN - Christmas Toys - Most Popular – 1954 - Yahtzee

GC729A - Welcome to Las Vegas

APPENDIX I – Geocache List

GC73FD - PASSING THE BUCK

GC74RRR - RT 66 - Amarillo - Cadillac Ranch II

GC75E90 - CP via NJ #1

GC75E98 - CP via NJ #2

GC764B5 - Lummis the Malpais Man

GC77ZZ0 - 4 Guys In A Car Visit Las Vegas

GC78FQW - UNDERCOVER Agent!

GC78YG3 - A Log for You to Log

GC79 - Iron Horse

GC79N8W - Y Knot Rest Here?

GC7B097 - Goin' up-ta-camp!

GC7B41E - KNP 2017 - La Source

GC7B7E3 - A Virtual Reward for a Dam Cool Dog

GC7BA4H - Reflection

GC7BM94 - Aloha from Hawaii

GC8209 - Historic Navajo Bridge

GC92 - Un-Original Stash

GC94DC - Daniel Boone Went UNDER a Mountain?

GCA7F1 - Marin Headlands One

GCAE2F - A Restful Stop in Ohio!

GCBD0A - Laughing Sal's

GCDE1 - Capitol View

GCDE41 - Micro Mead

GCE063 - Boulder City Virtual

GCEB2 - The view of an \Honest Man\

GCF2CD - Something to Crowe About

GCG2VN - LV Money-makers

GCG71X - Cadillac Ranch

GCGV0P - Original Stash Tribute Plaque

GCHDCZ - Living Large

GCHYED - Signs of the Times

GCJ8M8 - Auto Art

GCJKAC - Yellowstone Forever #2

GCJZDR - Cloud Gate aka The Bean

GCK25B - Geocaching Headquarters

GCKARJ - Go Rest A-man-a

GCKYV7 - Welcome To Florida

    GCMKWT - At the Pier

GCP5PM - No Rest for the Weary

GCQ14R - Welcome to North Carolina

GCTB8B - Stuffed Animals

GCVARM - Stop, Drop and Roll #4

APPENDIX I – Geocache List

GCW52P - A Barrel of Laughs

GCYCDF - LTL - Exit 451-Waterville Road

GCYCEH - LTL - Exit 447-Hartford Tennessee

APPENDIX II – Notable Cities / Our Route

On a trip that covers the amount of distance we covered, it's pretty easy to get lost in all of the various locations we passed through. When discussing this trip, I am often asked what route we took to be able to get all of the states in a single trip along with what some of the more notable places were. This section provides a bit more detail on where we actually were and how we got there.

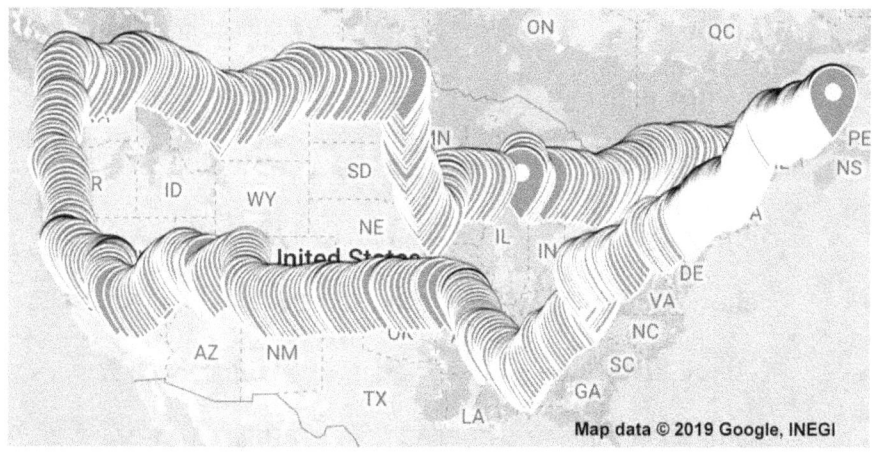

Cities / Towns / Villages / Locations

- Moncton, NB
- Saint John, NB
- Calais, ME
- Bangor, ME
- Portland, ME
- Portsmouth, NH
- Bennington, VT
- Albany, NY

APPENDIX II – Notable Cities / Our Route

- Buffalo, NY
- Erie, PA
- Cleveland, OH
- Elkhart, IN
- Chicago, IL
- Pleasant Prairie, WI
- Iowa City, IA
- Cameron, MO
- Elmwood, KS
- Omaha, NE
- Watertown, SD
- Fargo, ND
- Billings, MT
- Yellowstone Park, WY
- Kellogg, ID
- Seattle, WA
- Portland, OR
- San Francisco, CA
- Bakersfield, CA
- Las Vegas, NV
- Beaver Dam, AZ
- St. George, UT
- Cortez, CO
- Albuquerque, NM
- Amarillo, TX
- Oklahoma City, OK
- Little Rock, AK
- Transylvania, LO
- Jackson, MS
- Mobile, AB
- Pensacola, FL
- Atlanta, GA
- Greenville, SC
- Flat Rock, NC
- Knoxville, TN
- Middleboro, KY
- Princeton, WV
- Strasburg, VA
- Washington, D.C.
- Baltimore, MD
- Wilmington, DE
- New Brunswick, NJ

- New York City, NY
- New Haven, CT
- Providence, RI
- Foxborough, MA

www.ingramcontent.com/pod-product-compliance
Lightning Source LLC
Chambersburg PA
CBHW050551300426
44112CB00013B/1871